LADYSCAPING

BISPUBLISHERS

Design: Vetro Editions
www.vetroeditions.com

Illustrations: Caroline Selmes
Text: John Z. Komurki

© 2015 English edition BIS Publishers, Amsterdam
© 2015 Original Italian edition *Pussycut*, 24 ORE Cultura Srl, Milan

BIS Publishers
Building Het Sieraad
Postjesweg 1
1057 DT Amsterdam
The Netherlands
www.bispublishers.com
bis@bispublishers.com

ISBN 978-90-6369-406-7

ILLUSTRATIONS
Caroline Selmes

LADYSCAPING

A Girl's Guide to Personal Topiary

A Short Introduction
TO
Personal Topiary

In 1986, Jocely, Jonice, Janea, Joyce, Jussara, Juracy, and Judseia Padilha moved to Manhattan and opened a nail bar: the J Sisters Salon. It's bikini weather all year round in Victoria, the city on the Brazilian coast where the sisters grew up, and most women would wax off all their pubic hair on a regular basis; after they started offering this novel service ('the Brazilian') at the J Sisters Salon in 1994, it quickly became a craze that gripped celebrities and norms alike, and culminated in the 'Brazilian' episode of *Sex and the City* in 2000. Since then the Brazilian wax has become such a commonplace that entomologists are predicting the imminent extinction of the pubic louse (seriously).

There are diverse factors behind the Brazilian's popularity, one of them no doubt being porn's sudden, irrevocable ubiquity. But the pool-ball-bald look is far from universal: in Japan and South Korea, on the contrary, more and more women are having hair transplant operations to *increase* the spread and thickness of their bush, pubic hair standing for fertility and allure. And between the two extremes there lies an inexhaustible range of styles and approaches to the ancient question of pubic couture.

People have been trimming since the dawn of civilization. The first Egyptian cultures prized a smooth and hair-free body—both sexes shaved their heads and women rid themselves of their short-and-curlies with depilatory creams and a type of waxing process that involved oil and honey. The Ancient Greeks, too, prized marble smoothness: their representations of women are invariably hairless, where the men are not. Nor did the Romans value pubic hair. Young girls, it seems, started to remove it as soon as it sprouted, using tweezers called the 'volsella,' as well as 'philotrum' or 'dropax,' a depilatory cream made from a combination of picturesque ingredients, among them pitch, donkey fat, bat's blood, white vine or ivy gum extract, she-goat's gall, and powdered viper. Waxing with resin was also practiced.

Islamic culture is also notably anti-pubic, the Sunnah making clear that both men and women must shave at least once every forty days. This practice spread with the Muslim religion, and it is thought that the Crusaders brought it back to Europe, where it flourished all through the Renaissance. Indeed, it has been asked why the paintings of the great masters almost never show female pubic hair, and whether this represents an actual social practice or a general aesthetic principal. Whatever the case, the work of Michelangelo and Titian, of Bosch and Rubens, is full of porcelain-smooth vaginas. (There is a story that John Ruskin was horrified by his first experience of a real-life, hairy vagina, accustomed as he was to the unblemished pucker of classical art). Goya's *The Nude Maja* (1797) may be the first painting to depict female pubic hair (the artist was later hauled before the Inquisition for it), while Gustave Courbet's *L'Origine du monde* (1866) is surely the most notorious.

In the centuries following the Renaissance, it seems that European women's relation to their pubic hair varied over time and culture. Ever a taboo subject, we can only try to reconstruct contemporary attitudes from scattered pieces of evidence, such as the snuffbox in the museum at St. Andrew's University, Scotland, which contains the pubic hair of one of

King George IV's mistresses. Things changed radically with the advent of mass produced razors: when it launched its first razor for women in 1915, Gillette began to promote the idea that body hair was 'unsightly' and 'objectionable' and its removal 'feminine' and 'sanitary.' It was in 1915, too, that Harper's Bazaar magazine ran an image of a model in an evening gown that revealed her shoulders and hairless armpits. Since then, fashion and marketing have been locked into an ever more frantic competition to outdo each other in making women feel uncomfortable with their body hair. In most of America and Europe, leg and underarm shaving were already widespread by the 1930s. But it was the invention of the bikini in 1946 that marked the fluffy bush's death rang, and the 'bikini line' is but a hair away from a full-on sphinx.

Since that moment, then, there has been a continuous trend towards total hairlessness, with only a few backswings: the rise of Feminism led to a brief resurgence of genital hirsuteness, immortalized in the soft-focus mushroom clouds sported by Playboy and Penthouse models (Hugh Hefner referred to the rivalry between the two publications as 'The Pubic Wars'). And many groups and movements feel that, particularly for women, letting your pubic hair be is a way of rejecting hegemonic, often patriarchal, aesthetic and political values.

The revolution that kicked off at the J Sisters nail salon coincided with the sudden explosion of hardcore pornography into everyone's front room. There is now a whole generation of men who can attest to the effects of too much porn, particularly in terms of what it makes you come to expect. And one of the values that most pornography so insidiously promotes is that a vagina should always be fully shorn (just as an anus should always be impeccably pink, and reversible) to the point that for a lot of young people today, total genital hairlessness is the norm. One thing is clear: expressive pubic topiary has become this century's accessory of choice. Whatever your personal tastes or take on the question, there are many ways to wear your hair, and, however you do, your pubes will always say a lot about you.

TABLE OF CONTENTS

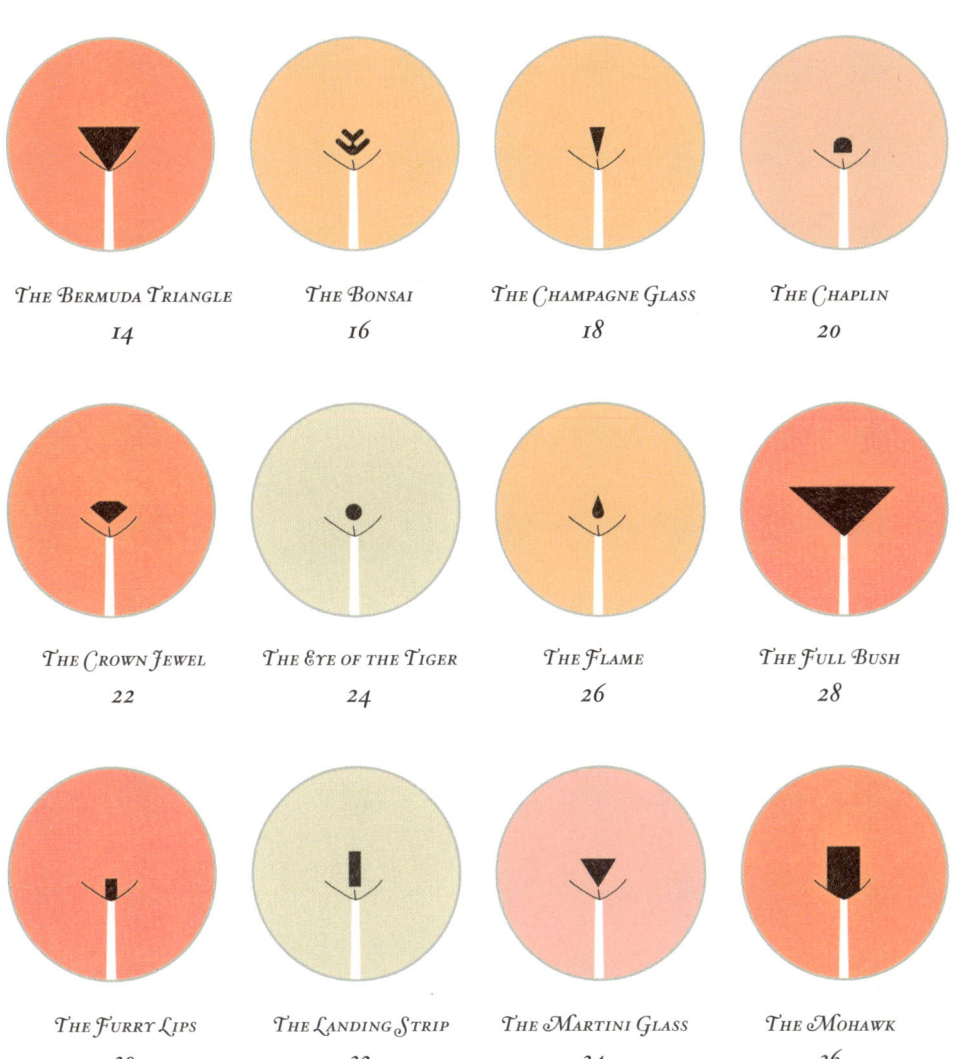

The Bermuda Triangle — 14
The Bonsai — 16
The Champagne Glass — 18
The Chaplin — 20
The Crown Jewel — 22
The Eye of the Tiger — 24
The Flame — 26
The Full Bush — 28
The Furry Lips — 30
The Landing Strip — 32
The Martini Glass — 34
The Mohawk — 36

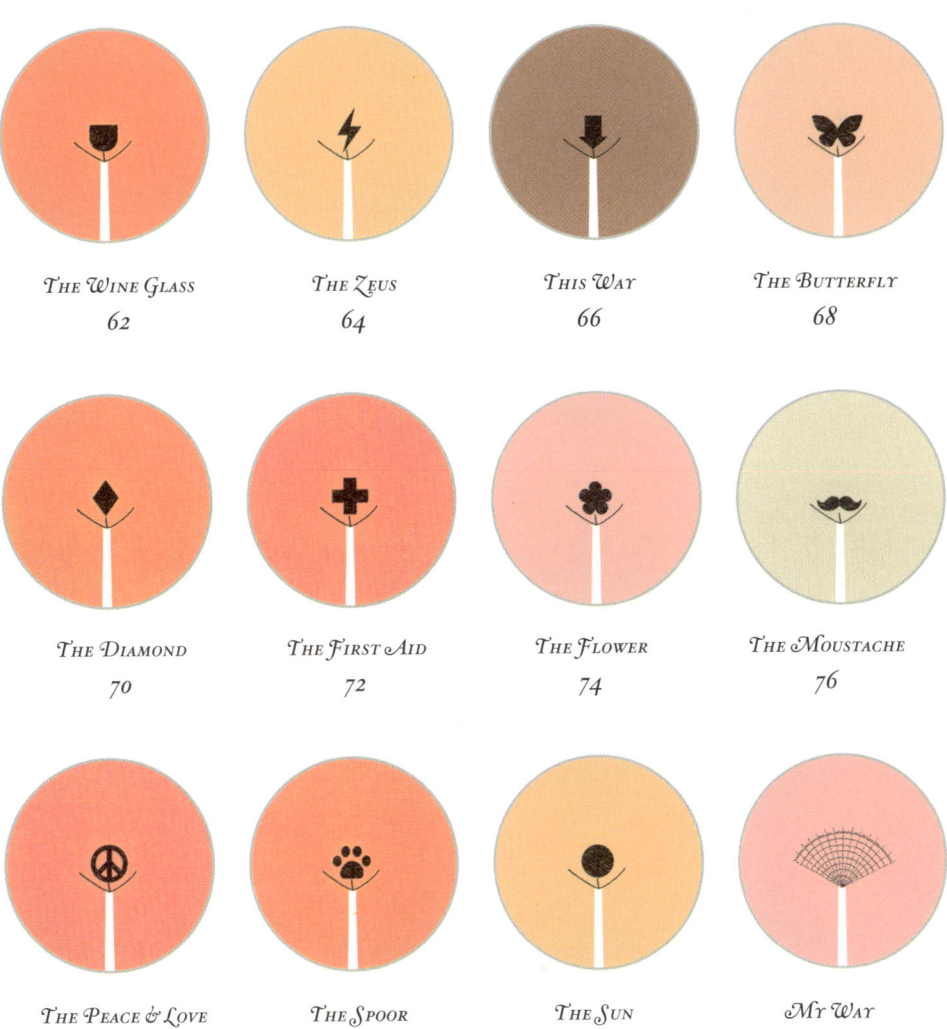

The Garden
ILLUSTRATED TABLES

THE BERMUDA TRIANGLE

"Luminous triangle! Whoever has not known you is without sense!"

                                    Comte de Lautreamont

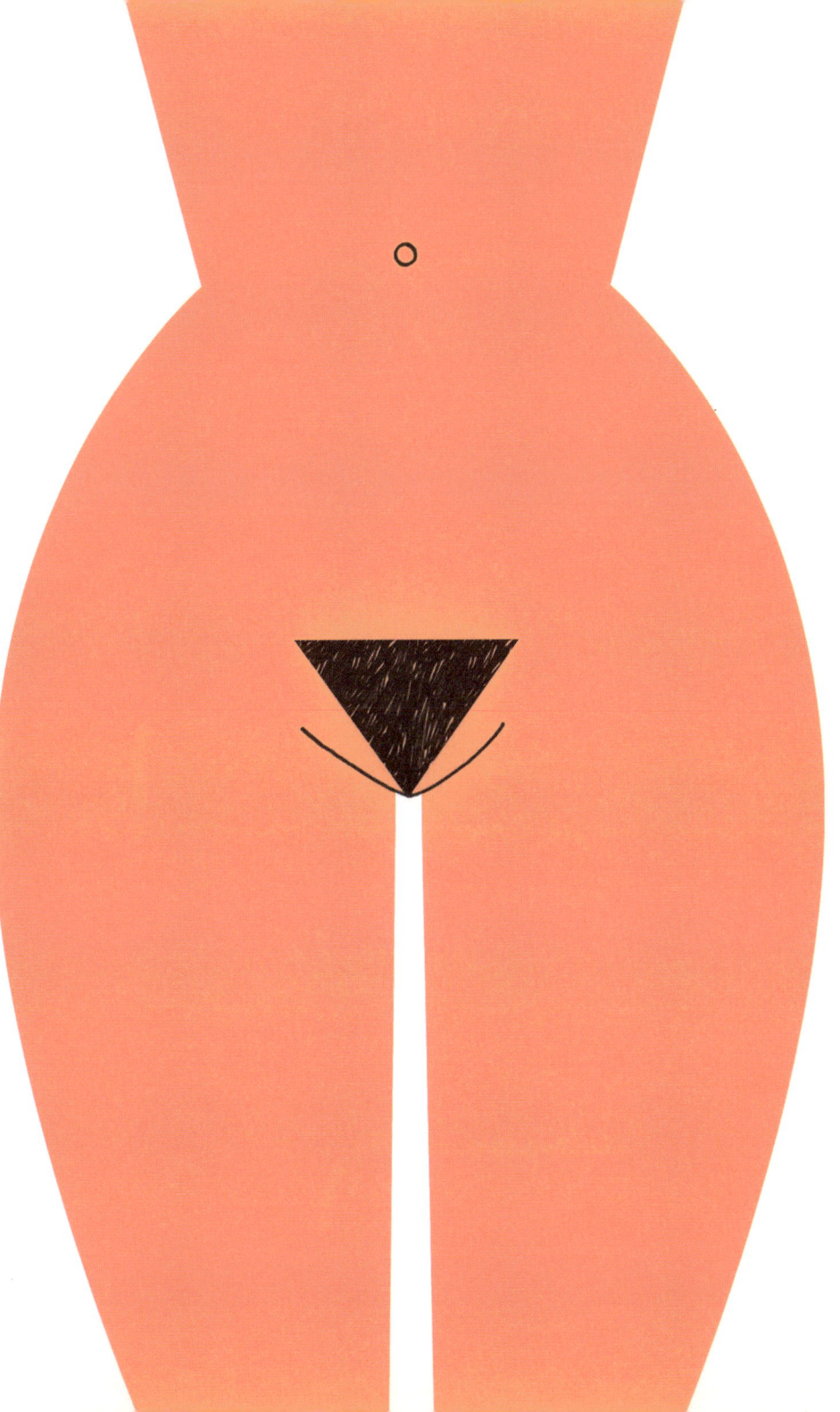

THE BONSAI

"Bonsai is not the result: that comes after. Your enjoyment is what is important."

　　　　　　　　　　　　John Naka

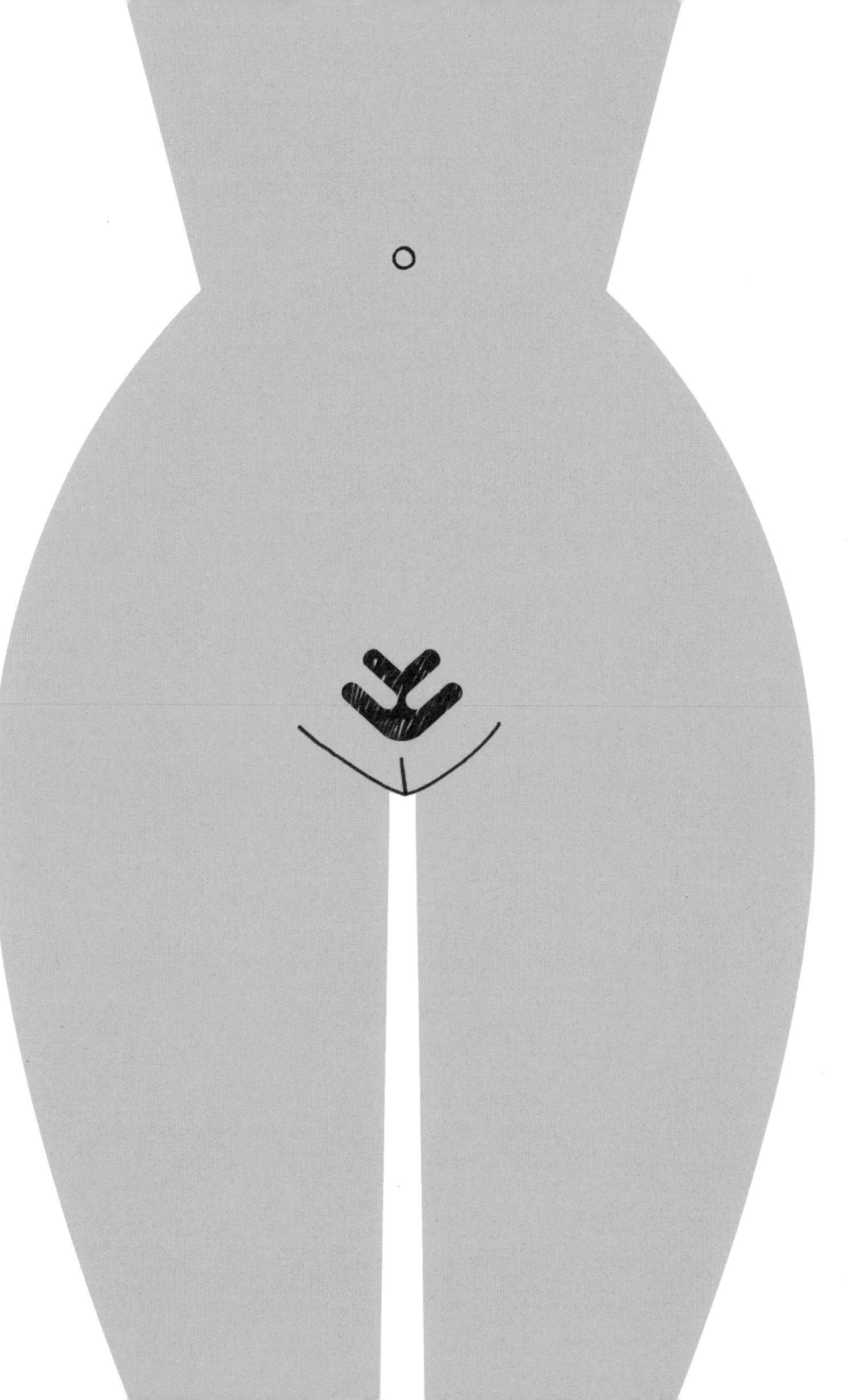

THE CHAMPAGNE GLASS

"Champagne is the only wine that enhances a woman's beauty."

                          Madame de Pompadour

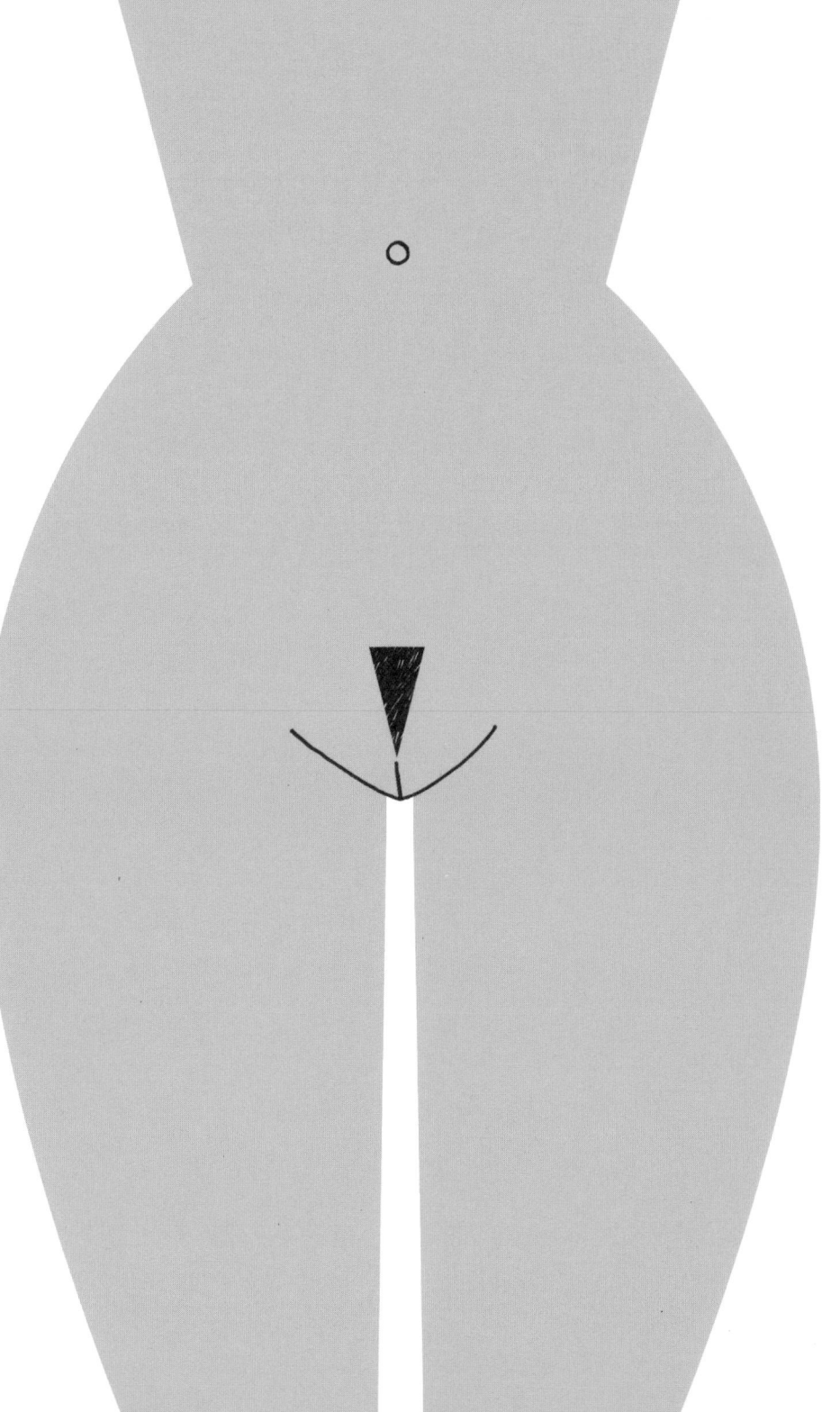

THE CHARLIE CHAPLIN

"What do you want meaning for?
Life is desire, not meaning."
                      Charles Chaplin

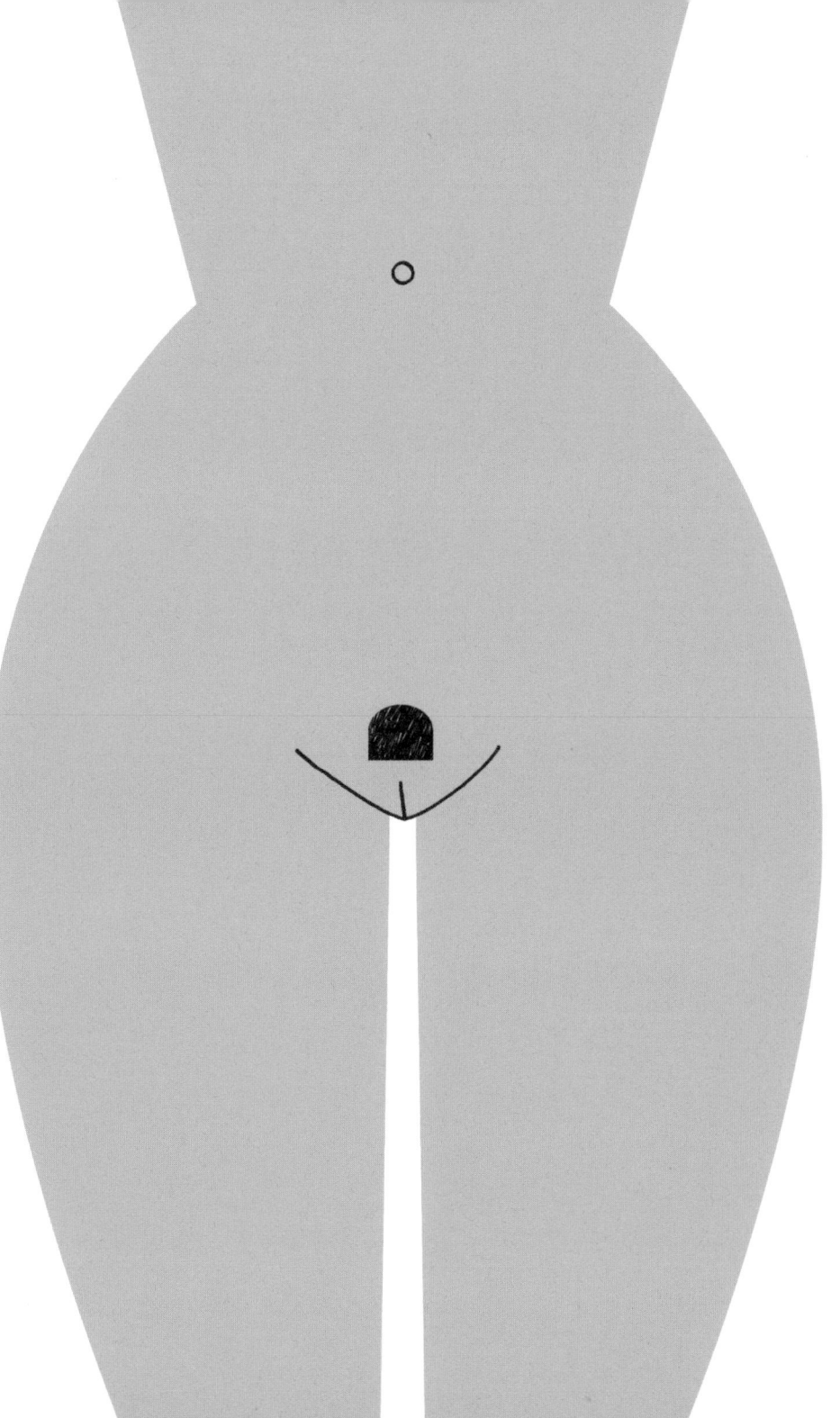

THE CROWN JEWEL

"For me, hair is an accoutrement. Hair is jewellery. it's an accessory."

Jill Scott

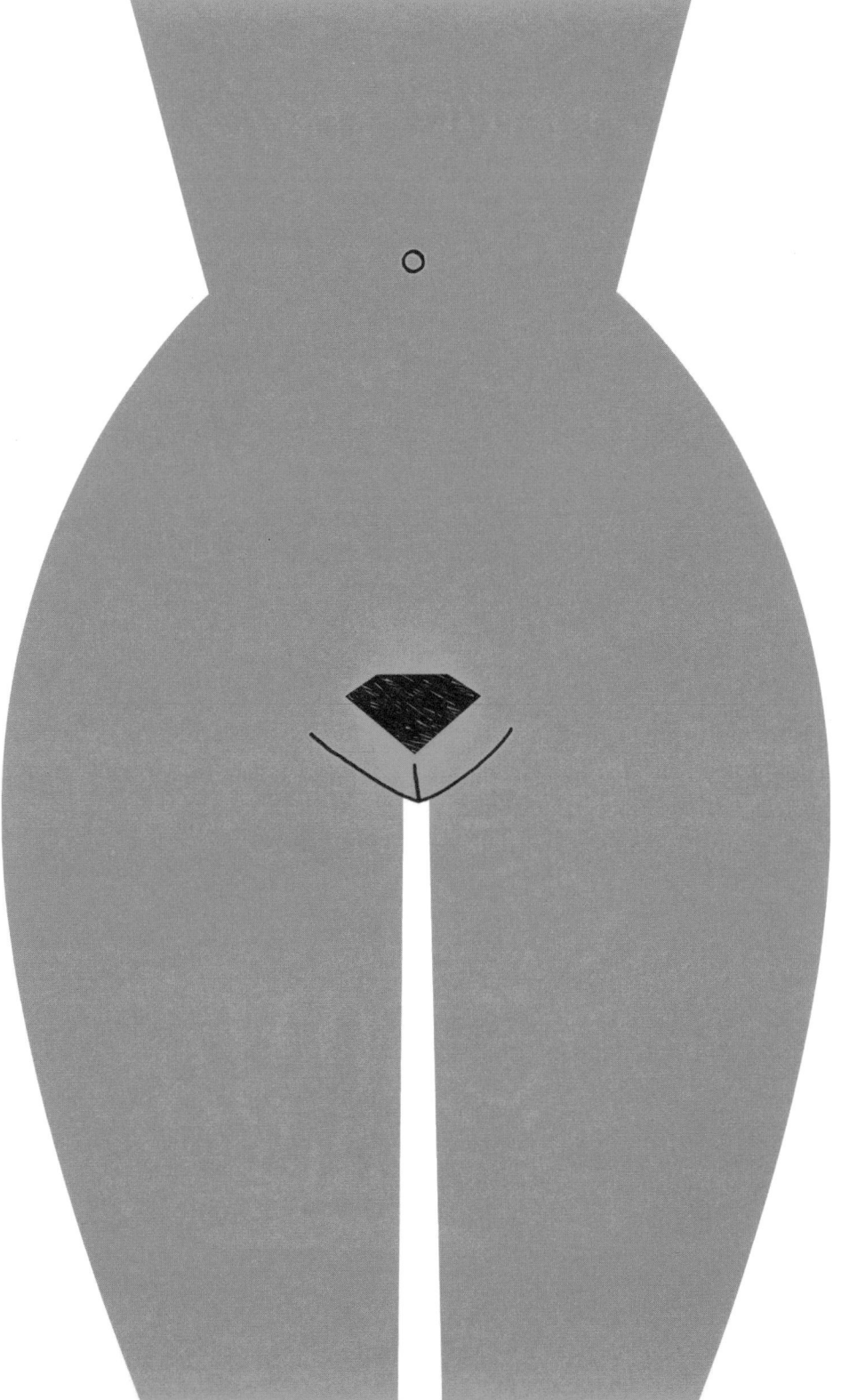

THE EYE OF THE TiGER

"in what distant deeps or skies
Burnt the fire of thine eyes."
            William Blake

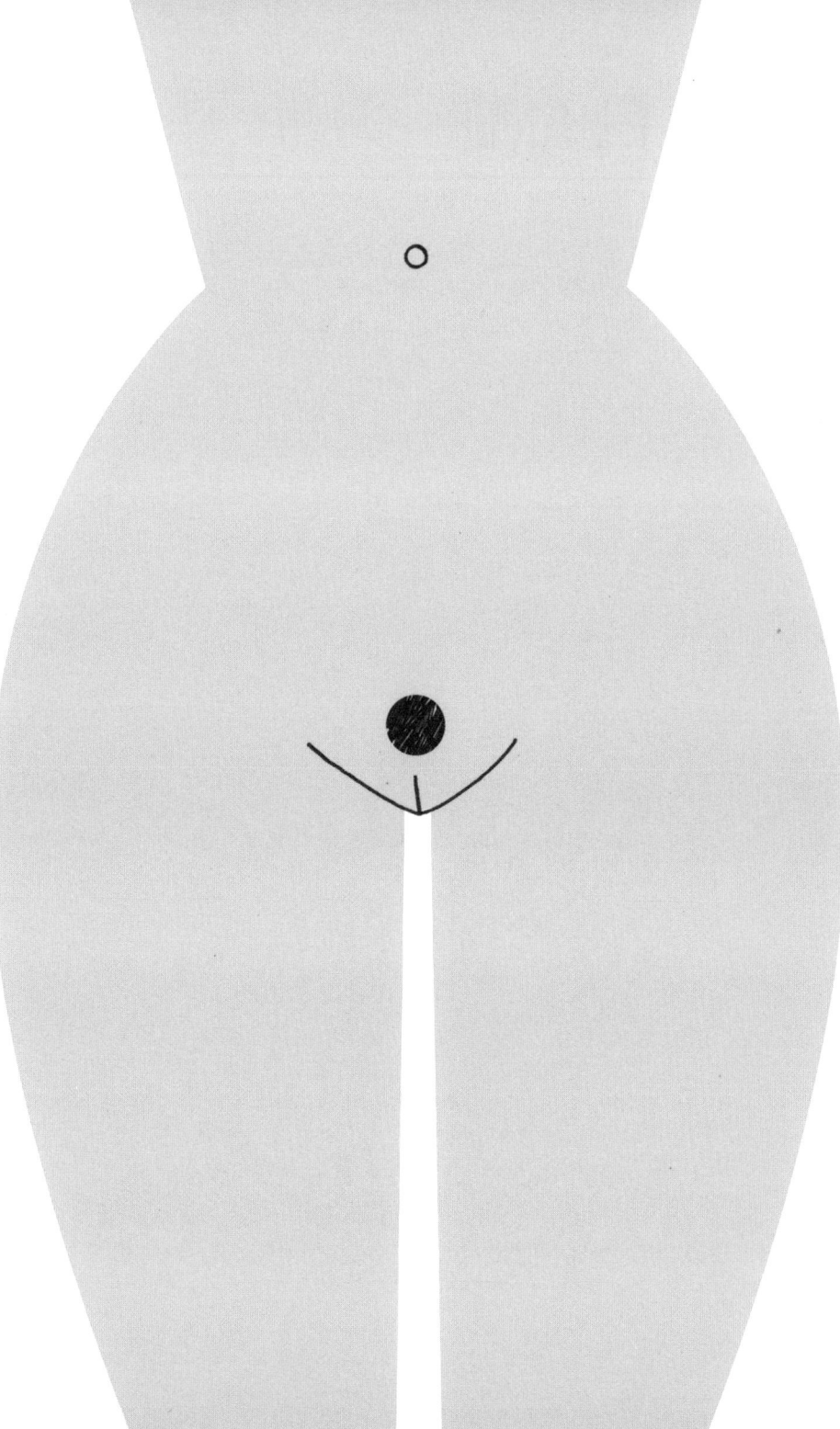

THE FLAME

"Burning in water, drowning in flame."
                    Charles Bukowski

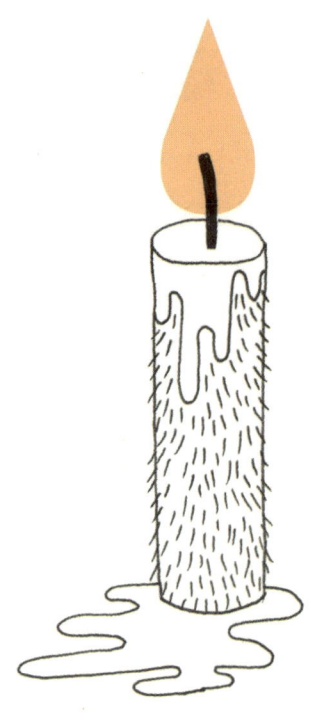

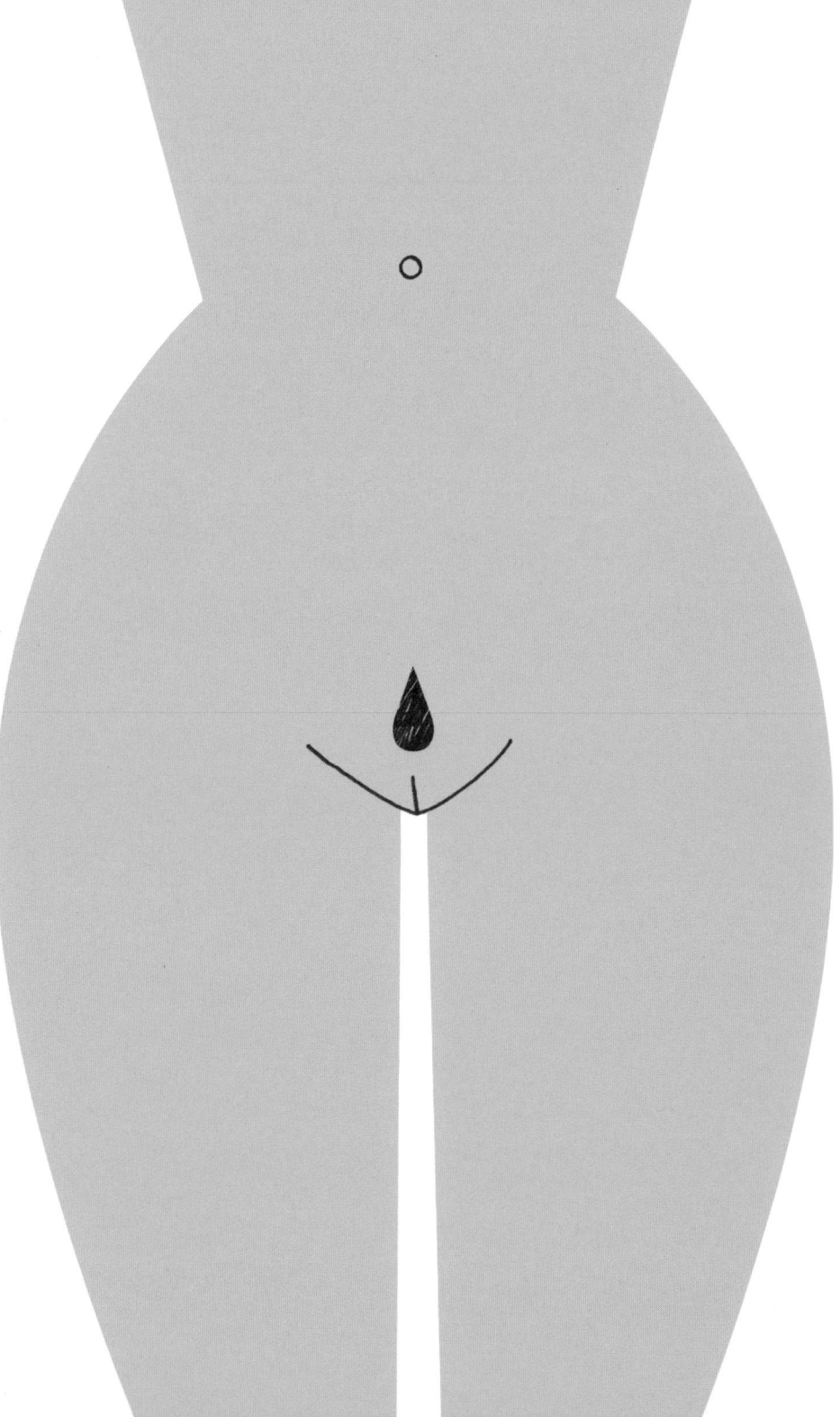

THE FULL BUSH

"To such an extent does nature delight and abound in variety that among her trees there is not one plant to be found which is exactly like another; and not only among the plants, but among the boughs, the leaves and the fruits, you will not find one which is exactly similar to another."

Leonardo da Vinci

THE FURRY LIPS

"The gentle sin is this: My lips, two blushing pilgrims, ready stand To smooth that rough touch with a tender kiss."

                                                Shakespeare

THE LANDiNG STRiP

"if you can walk away from a landing, it's a good landing. if you use the airplane the next day, it's an outstanding landing."

Chuck Yeager

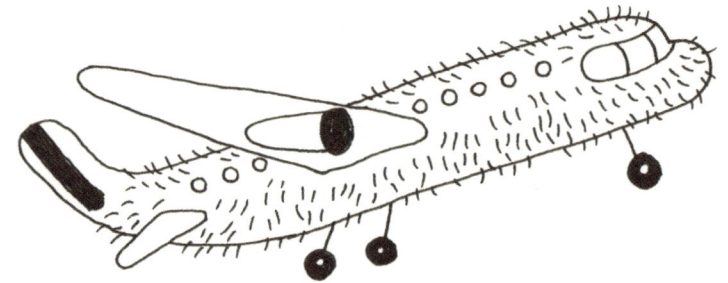

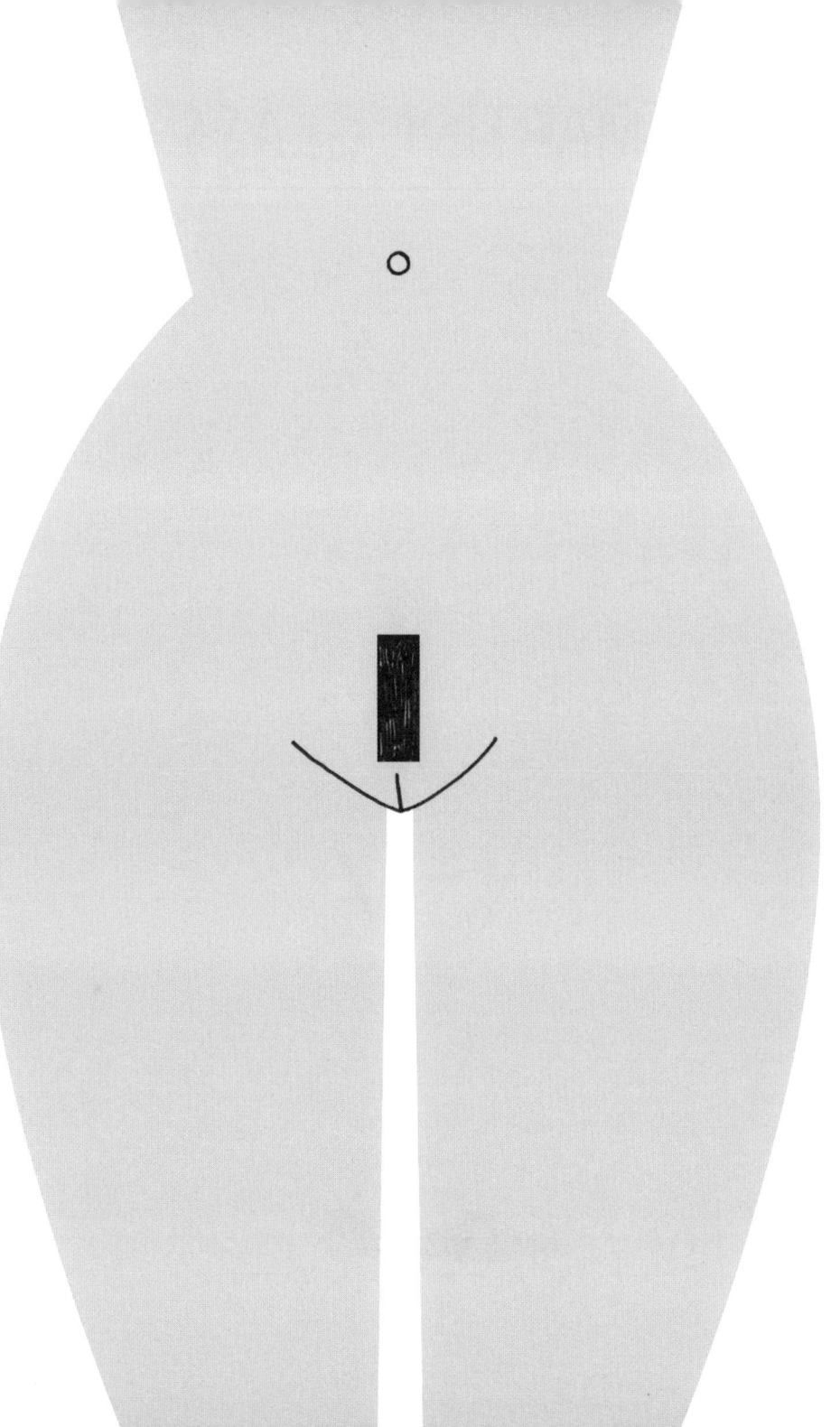

THE MARTINI GLASS

"Happiness is finding two olives in your Martini when you are hungry."

                        Johnny Carson

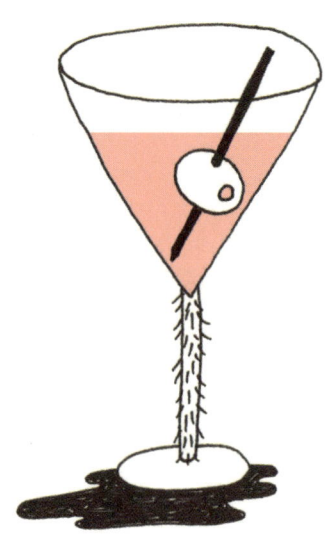

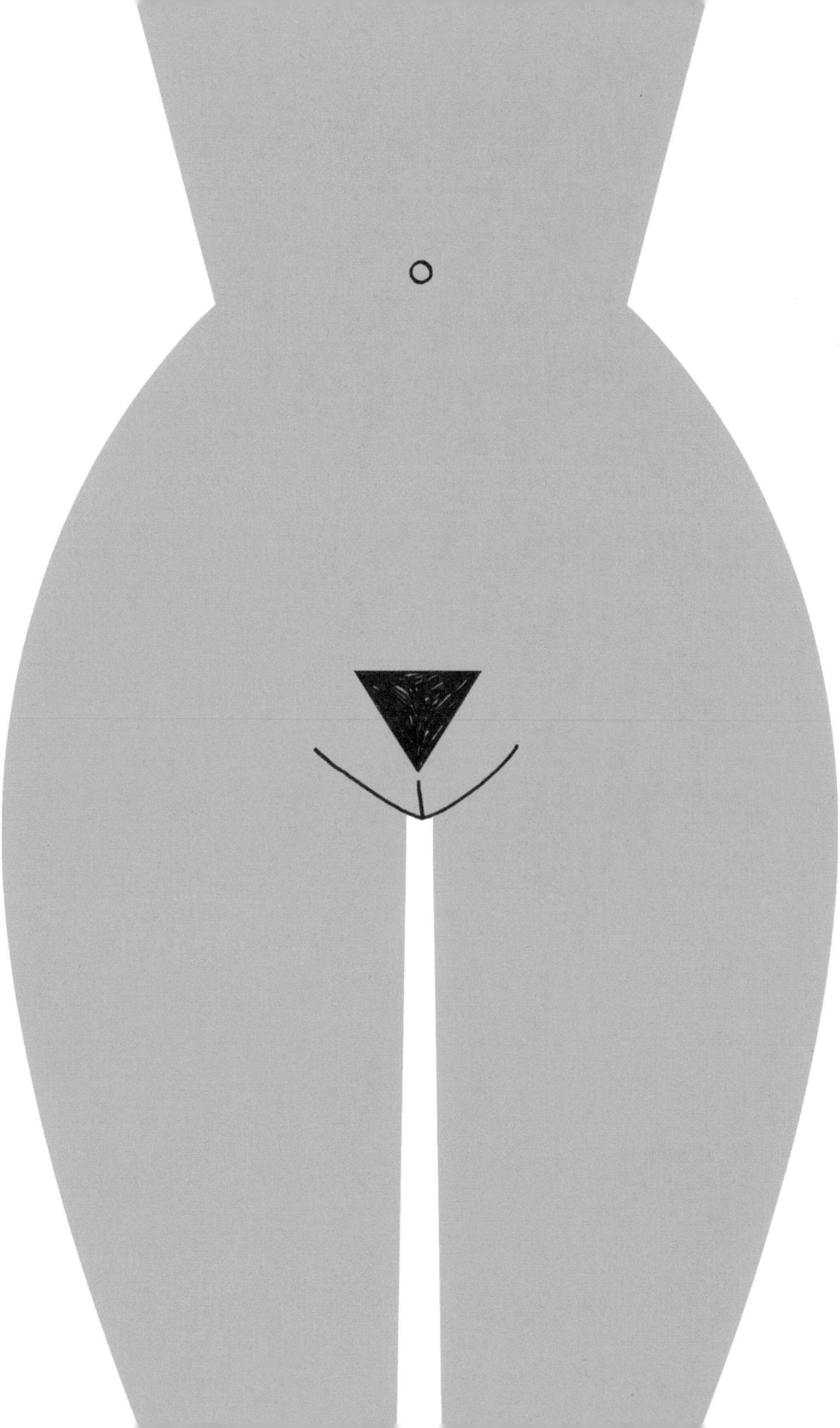

THE MOHAWK

"if he work the middle like a mohawk, tell 'em he can meet me where them girls say Aloha."

— Nicki Minaj

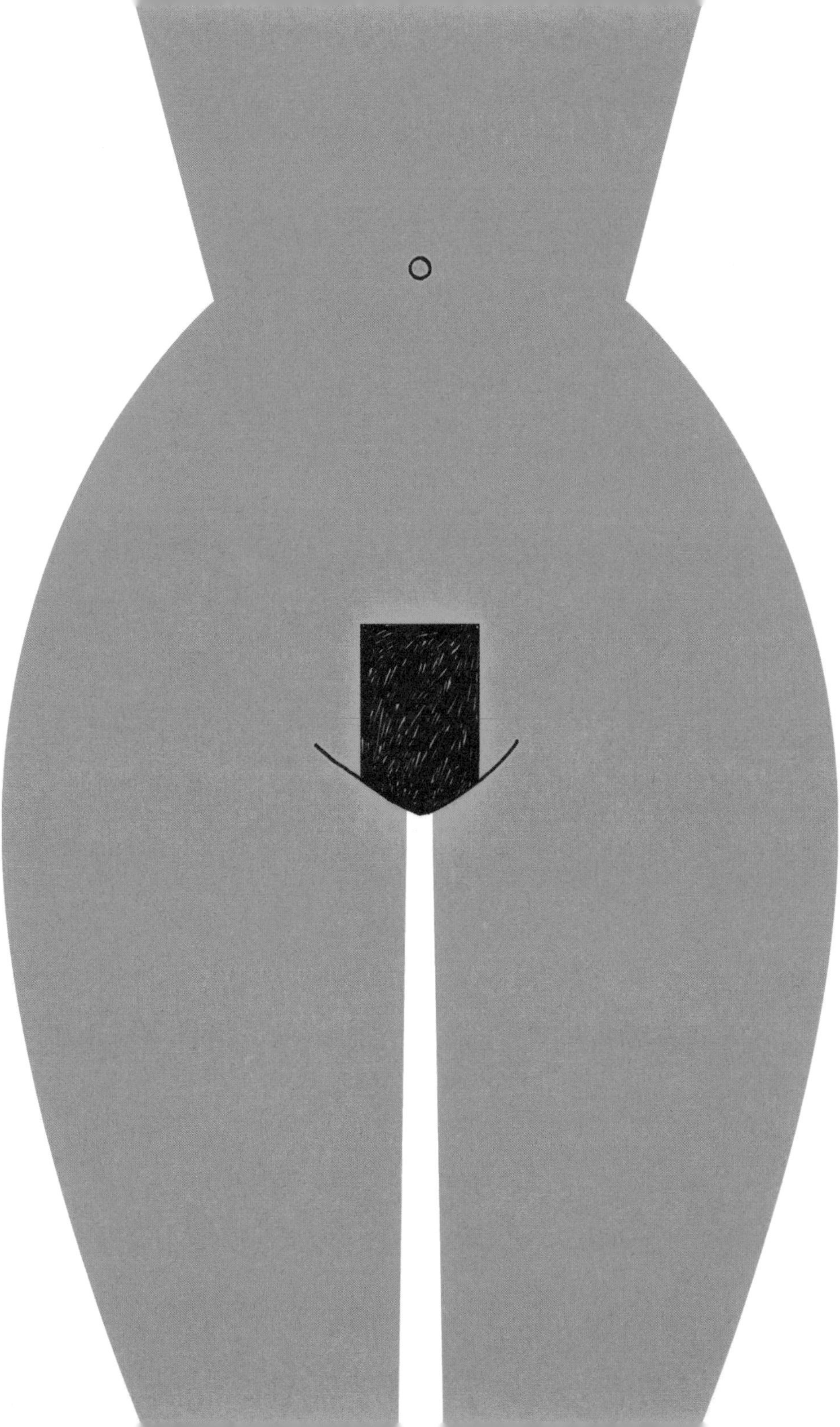

THE MOON

"Aim for the moon. if you miss, you may hit a star."

W. Clement Stone

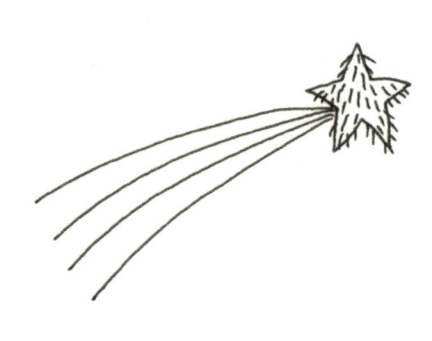

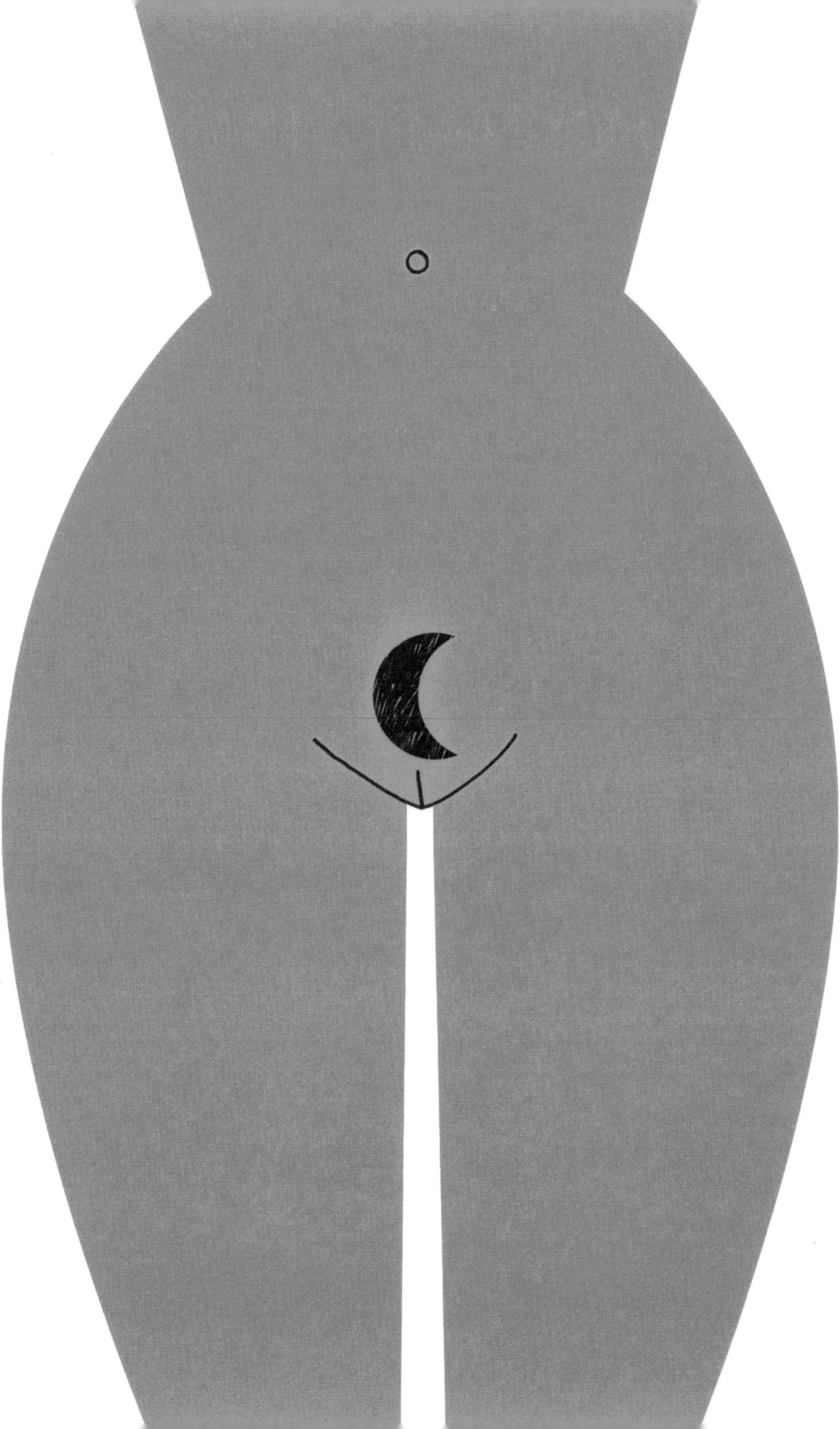

THE POSTAGE STAMP

"i should be a postage stamp, because that's the only way i'll ever get licked."

                              Muhammad Ali

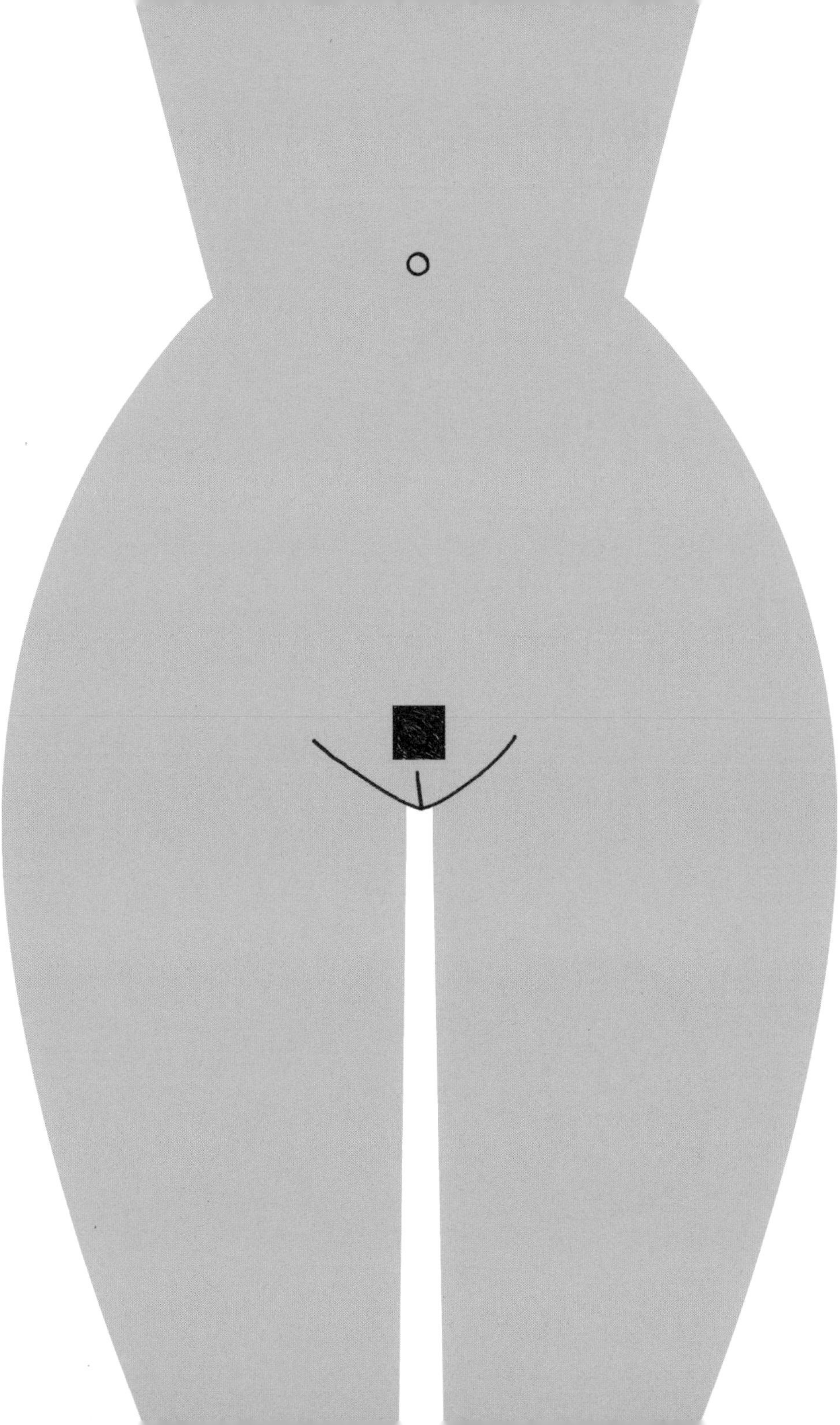

THE ROUND BUTTON

"A circle may be small, yet it may be as mathematically beautiful and perfect as a large one."

      isaac D'israeli

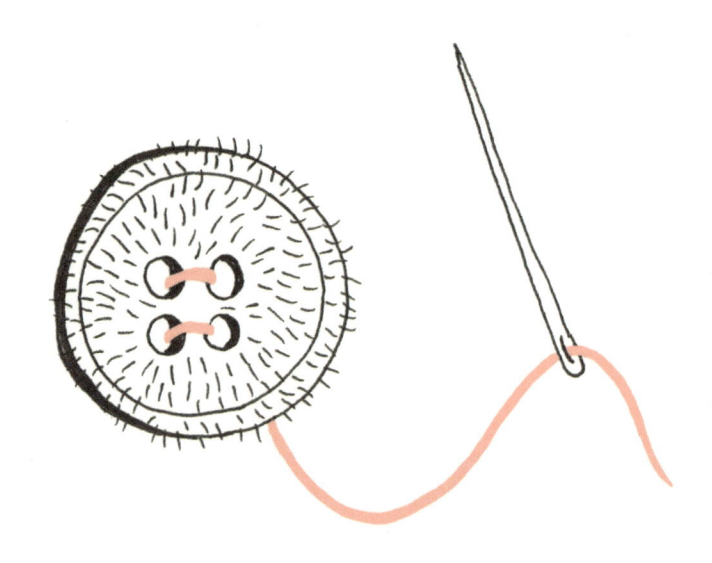

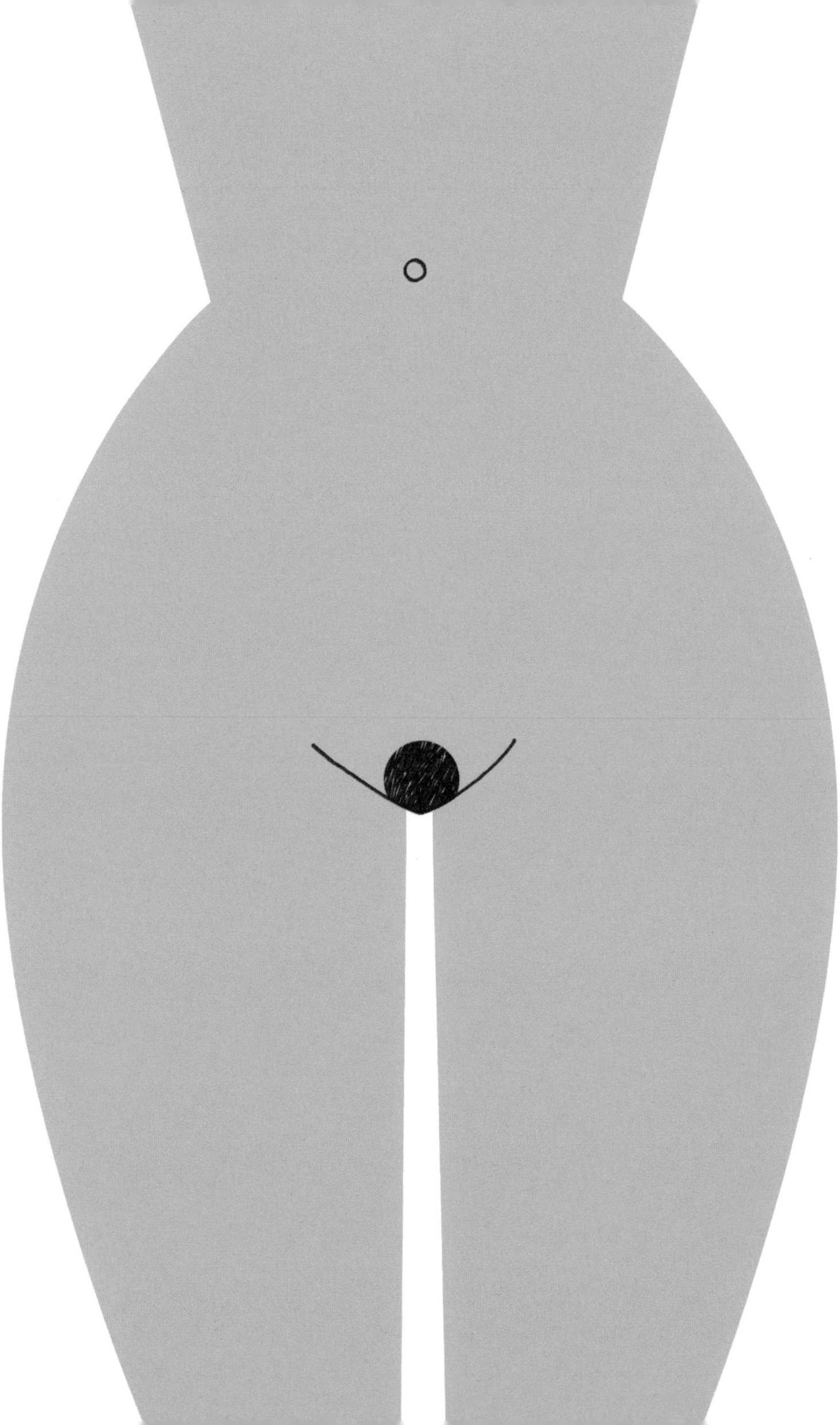

V FOR VENDETTA

"The ending is nearer than you think, and it is already written. All that we have left to choose is the correct moment to begin."

Alan Moore, V for Vendetta

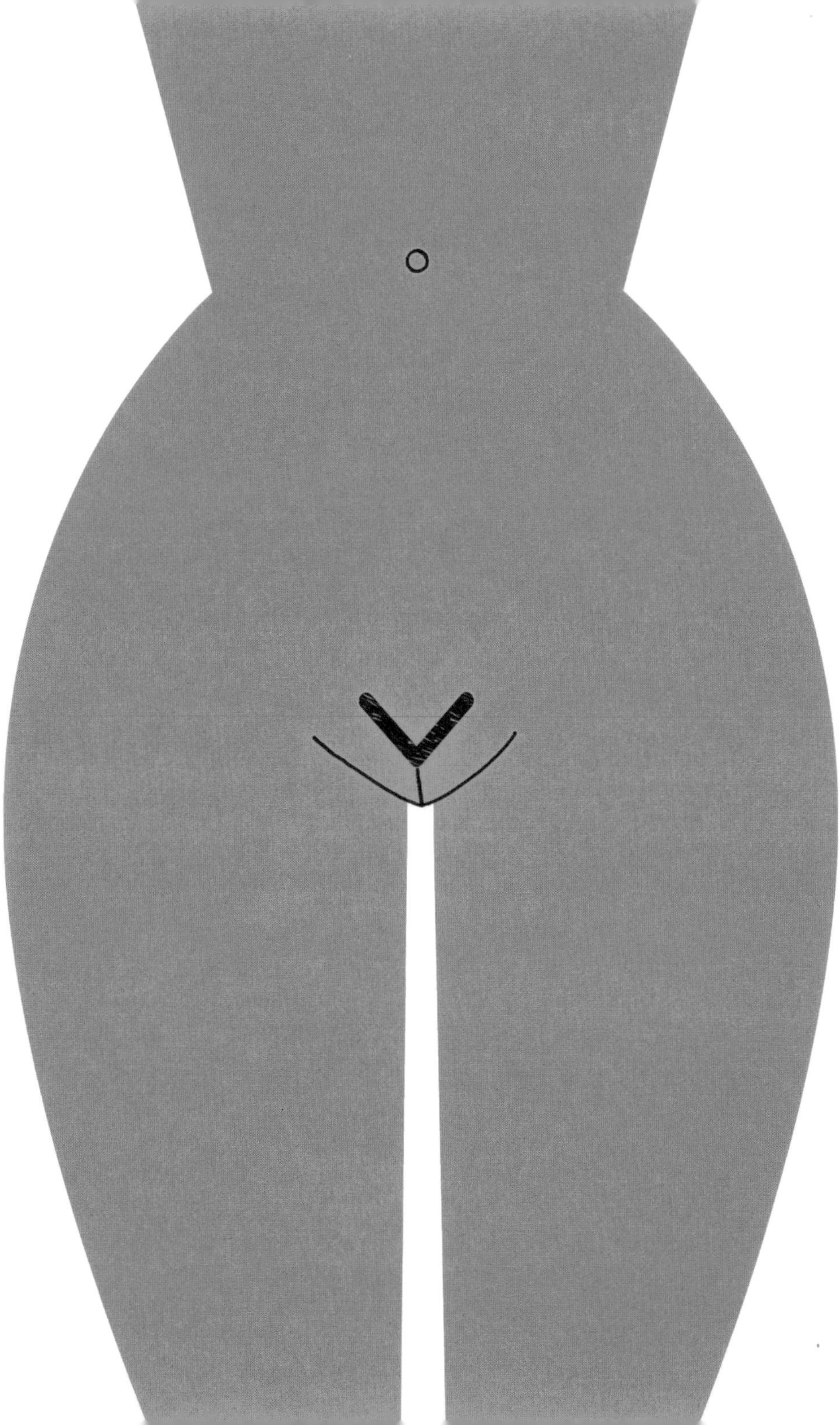

THE BIKINI

"A girl in a bikini is like having a loaded gun on your coffee table. There's nothing wrong with them, but it's hard to stop thinking about."

GARRISON KEILLOR

THE BRAZILIAN

"Bald as the bare mountain tops are bald, with a baldness full of grandeur."

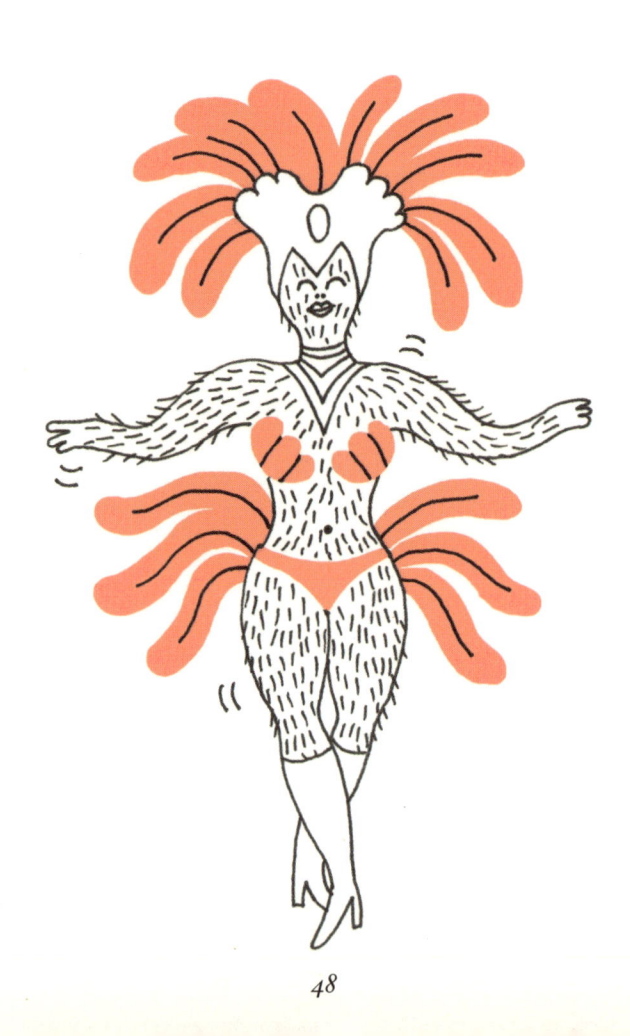

Matthew Arnold

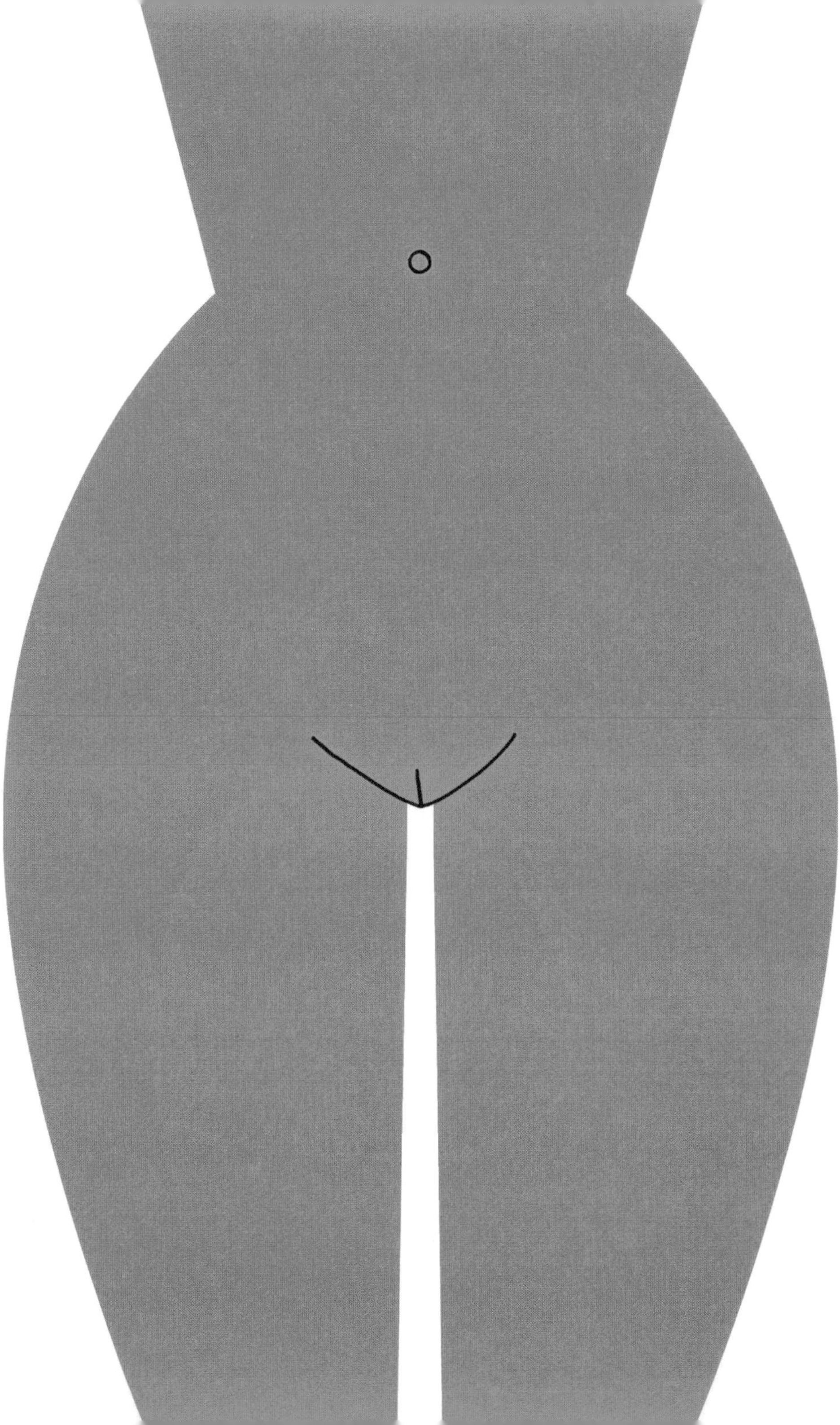

THE CLIT CAP

"Circles are praised, not that abound in largeness, but the exactly round."

Edmund Waller

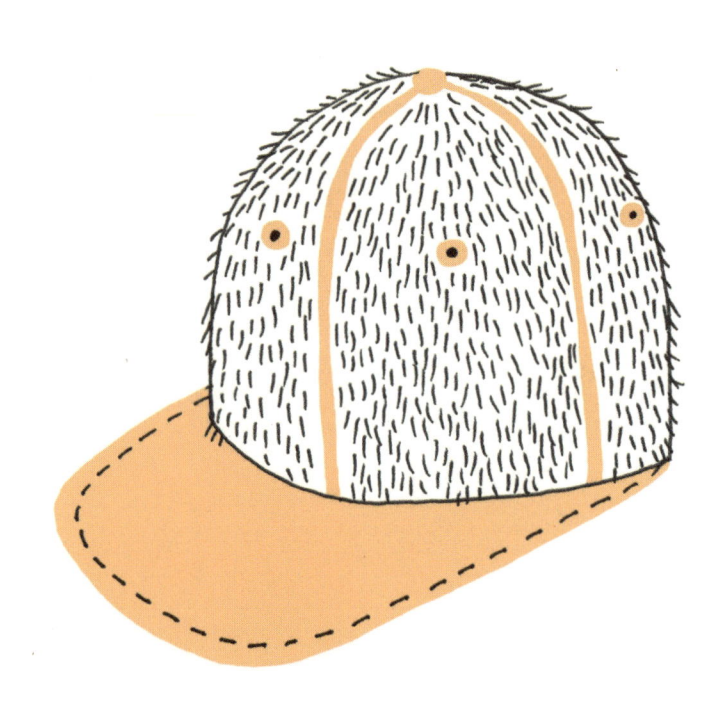

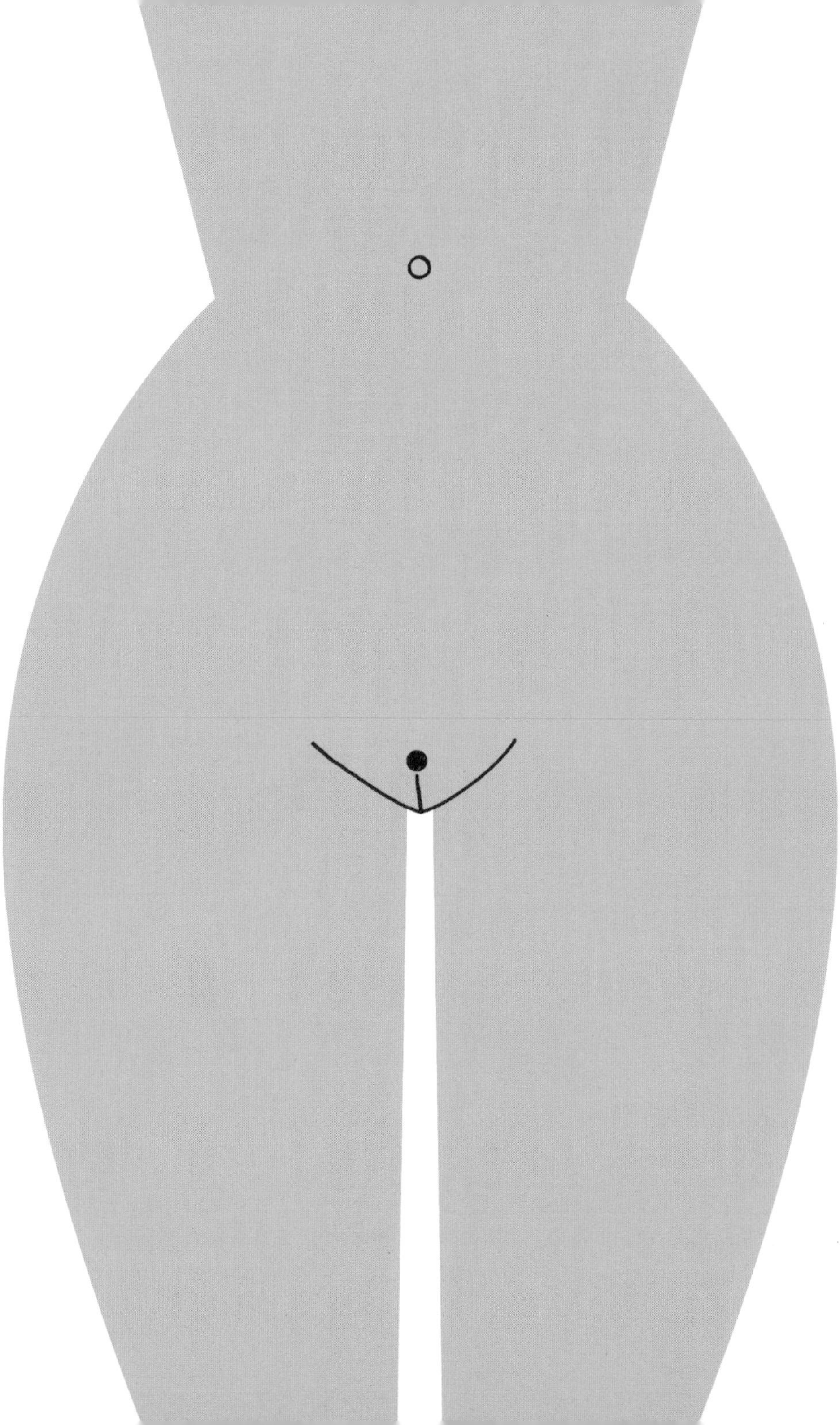

THE SWEET HEART

"And now here is my secret, a very simple secret: it is only with the heart that one can see rightly; what is essential is invisible to the eye."

Antoine de Saint Exupéry

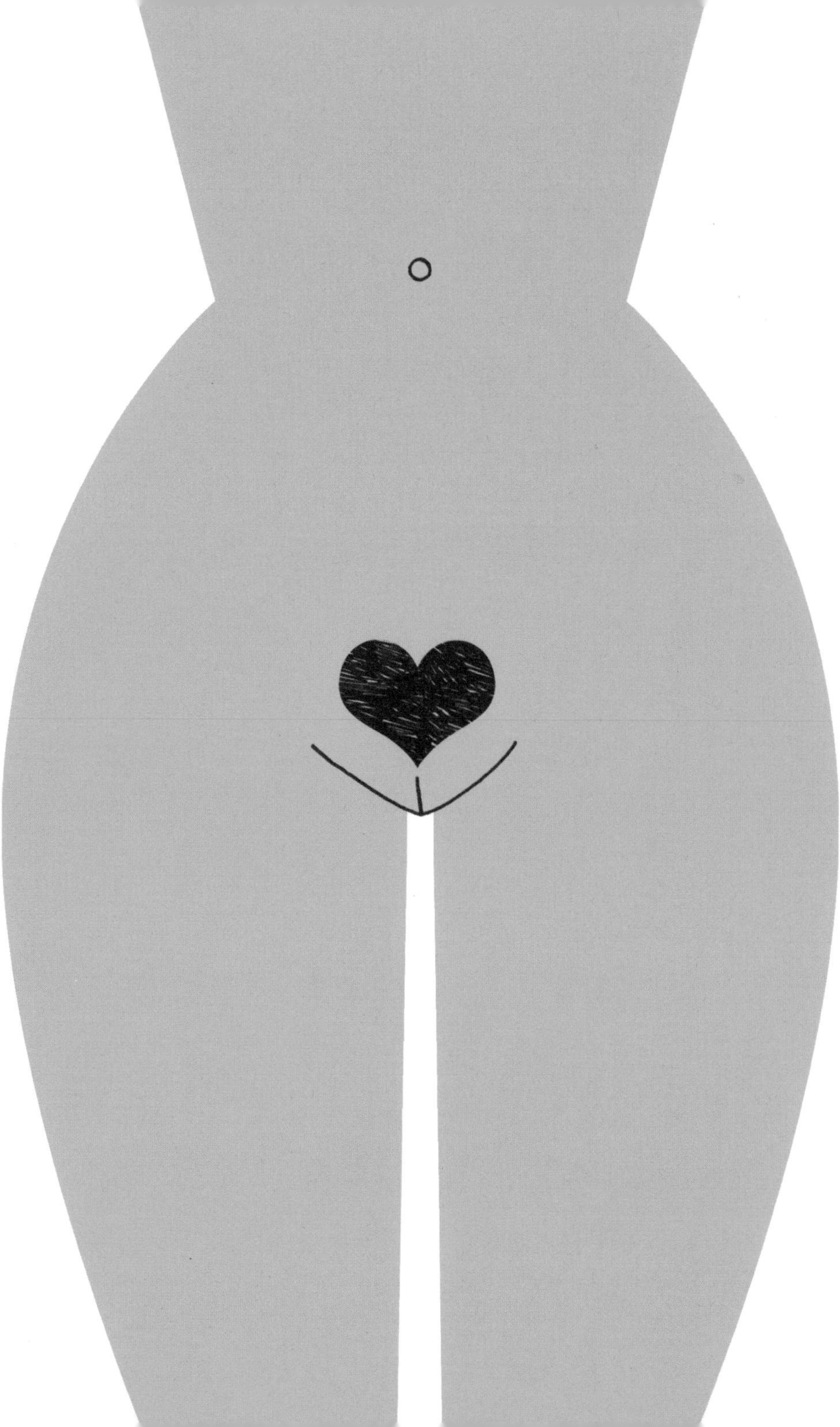

THE LONG LINE

"There is nothing in a caterpillar that tells you it's going to be a butterfly."

R. Buckminster Fuller

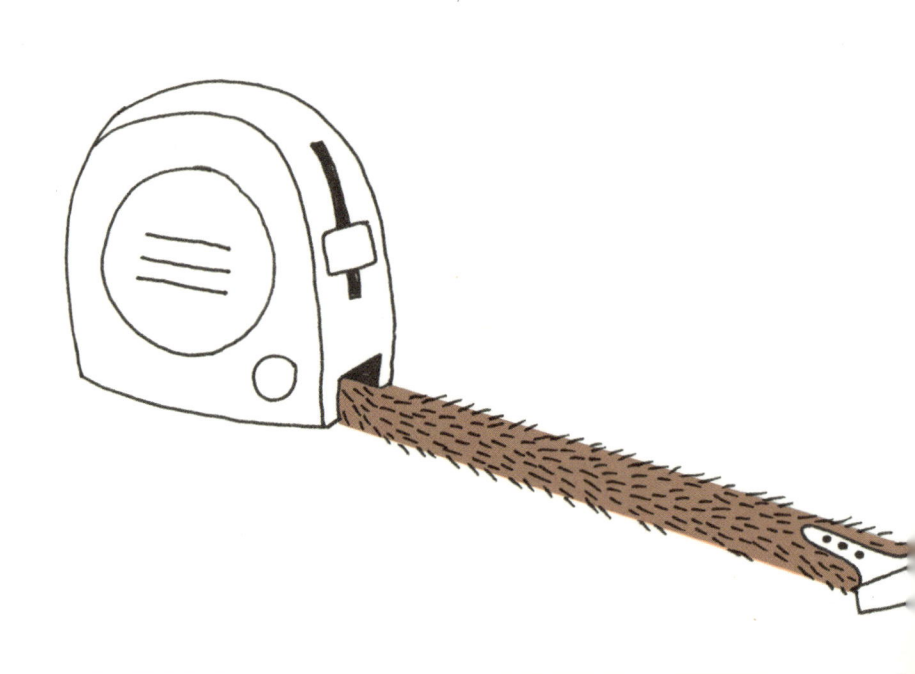

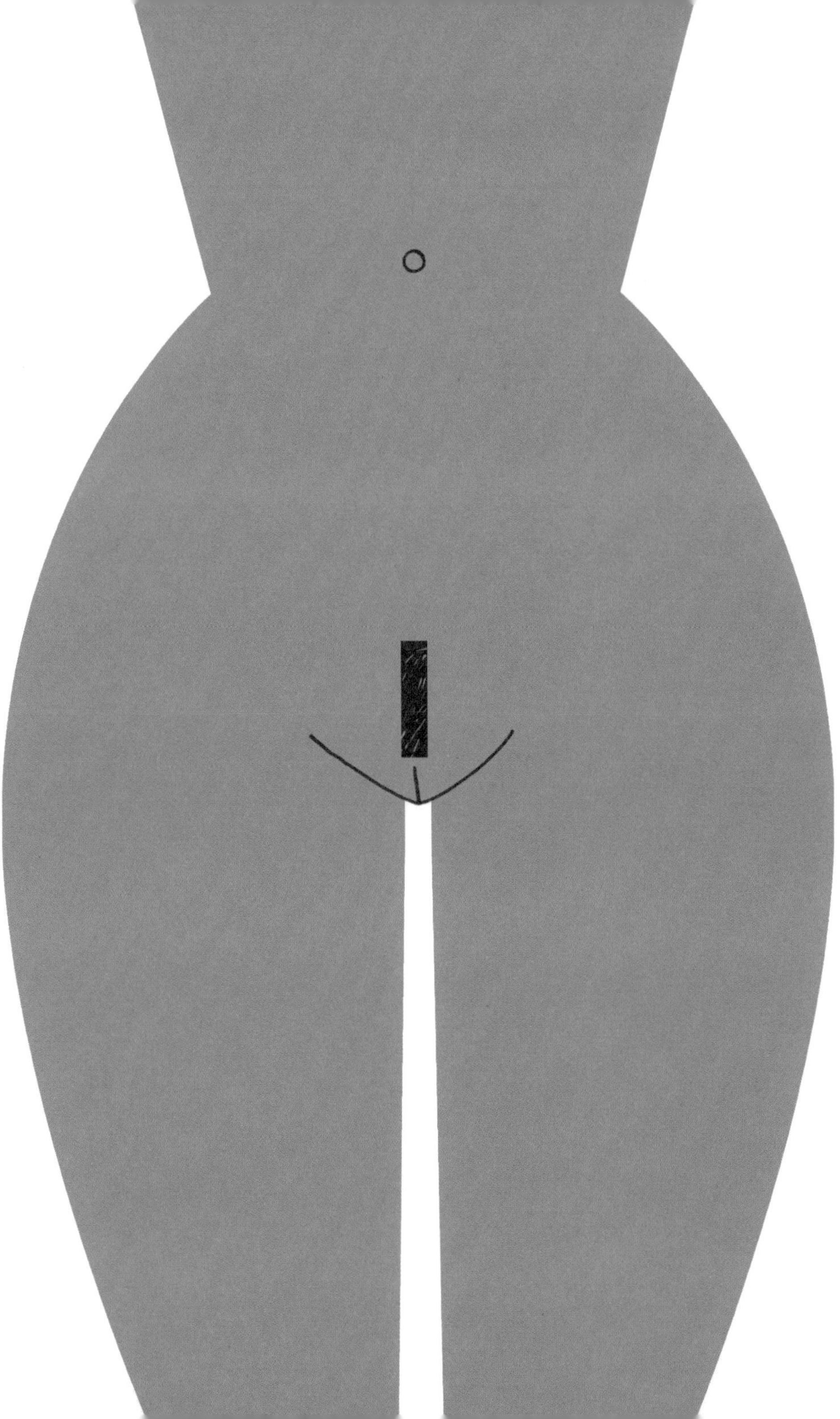

THE PENCIL

"I am a little pencil in the hand of a writing god who is sending a love letter to the world."
                                    Mother Teresa

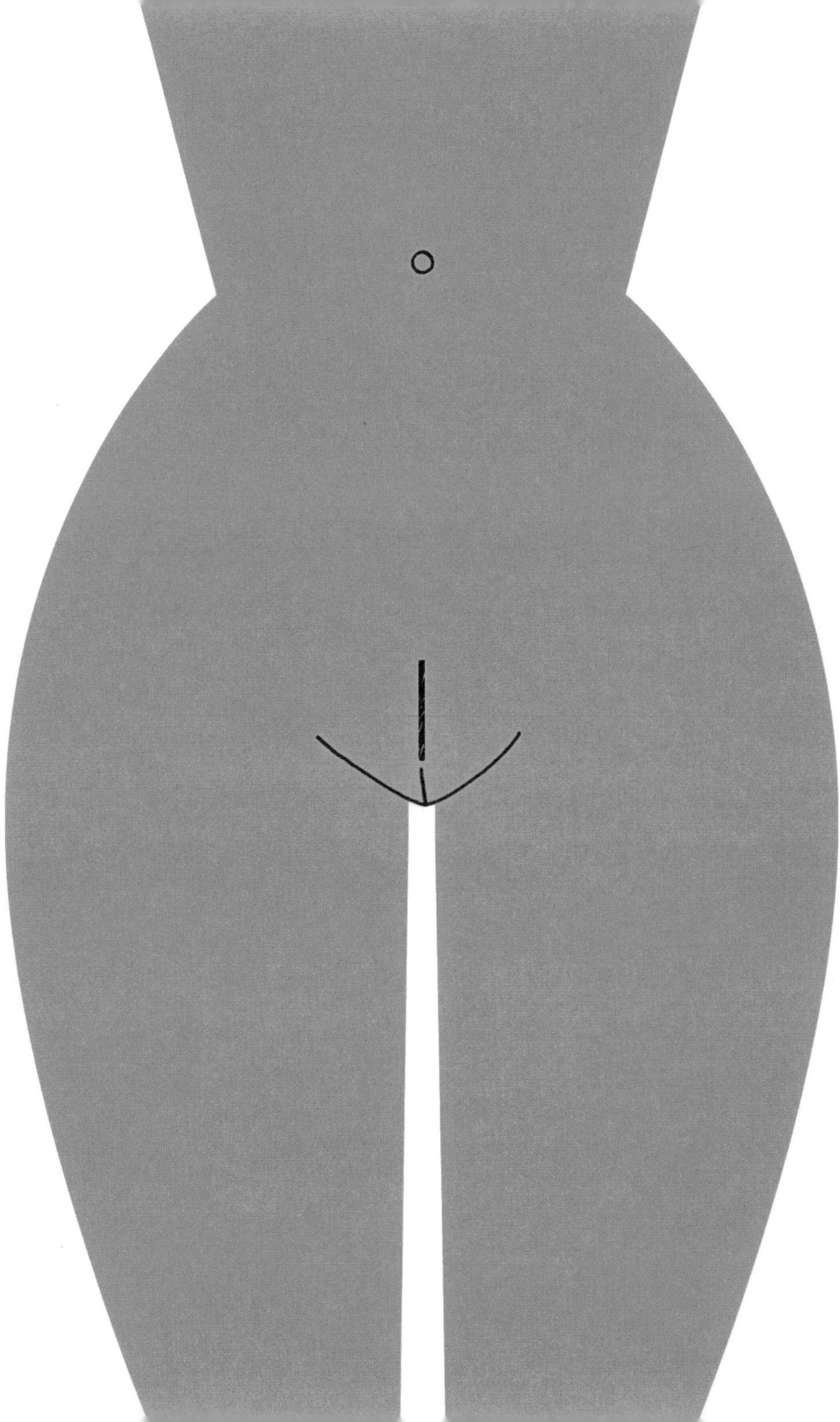

THE SQUARE

"Once i am in the square circle, i am in my home."
                                        Floyd Mayweather, Jr.

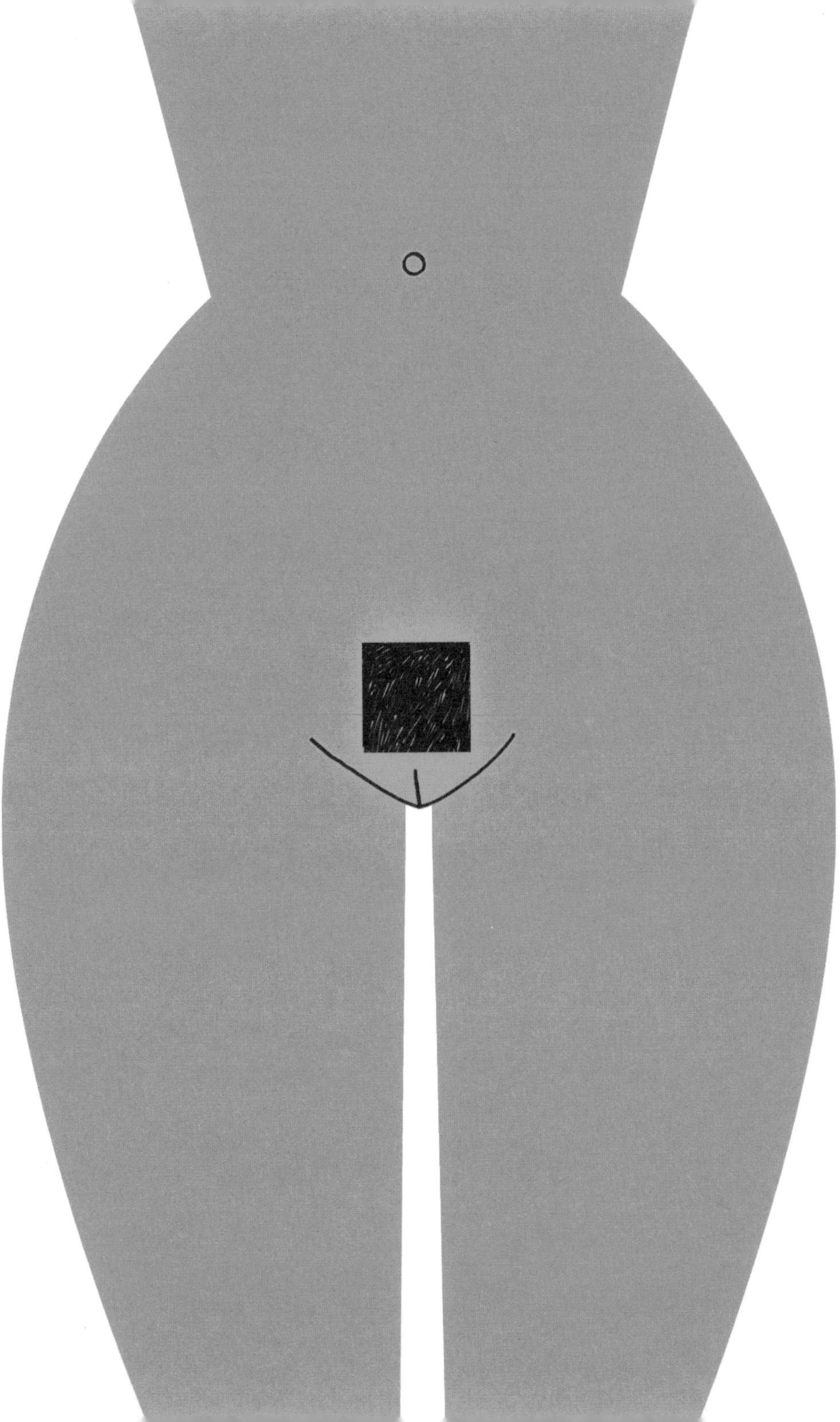

THE STAR

"We are all in the gutter, but some of us are looking at the stars."

Oscar Wilde

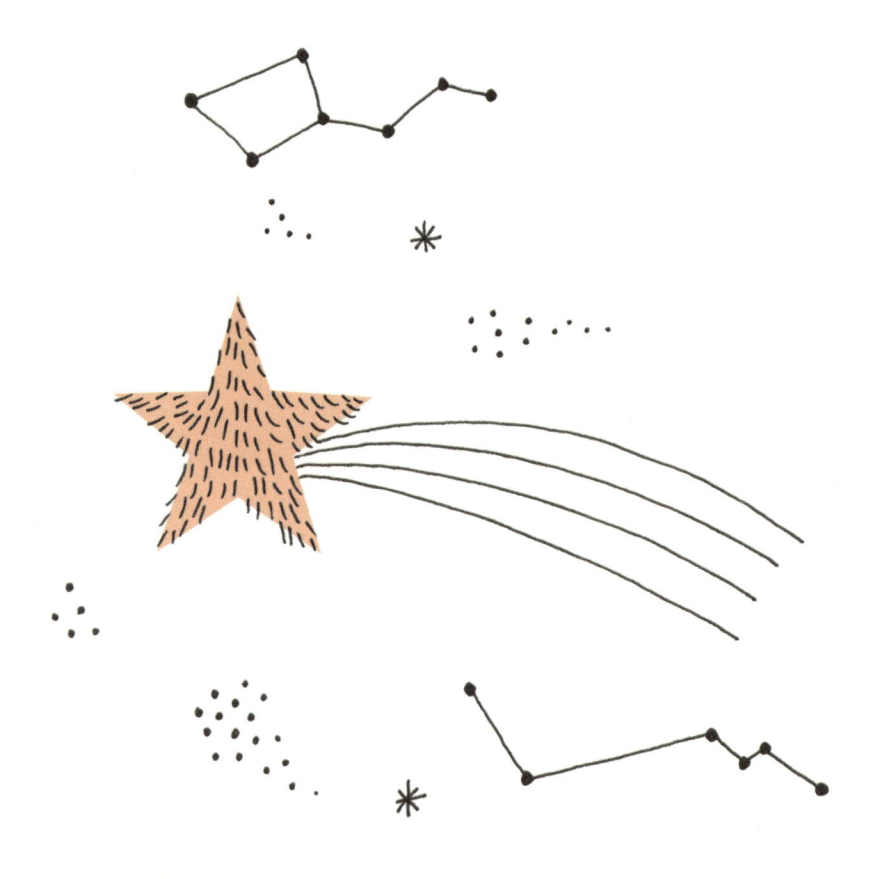

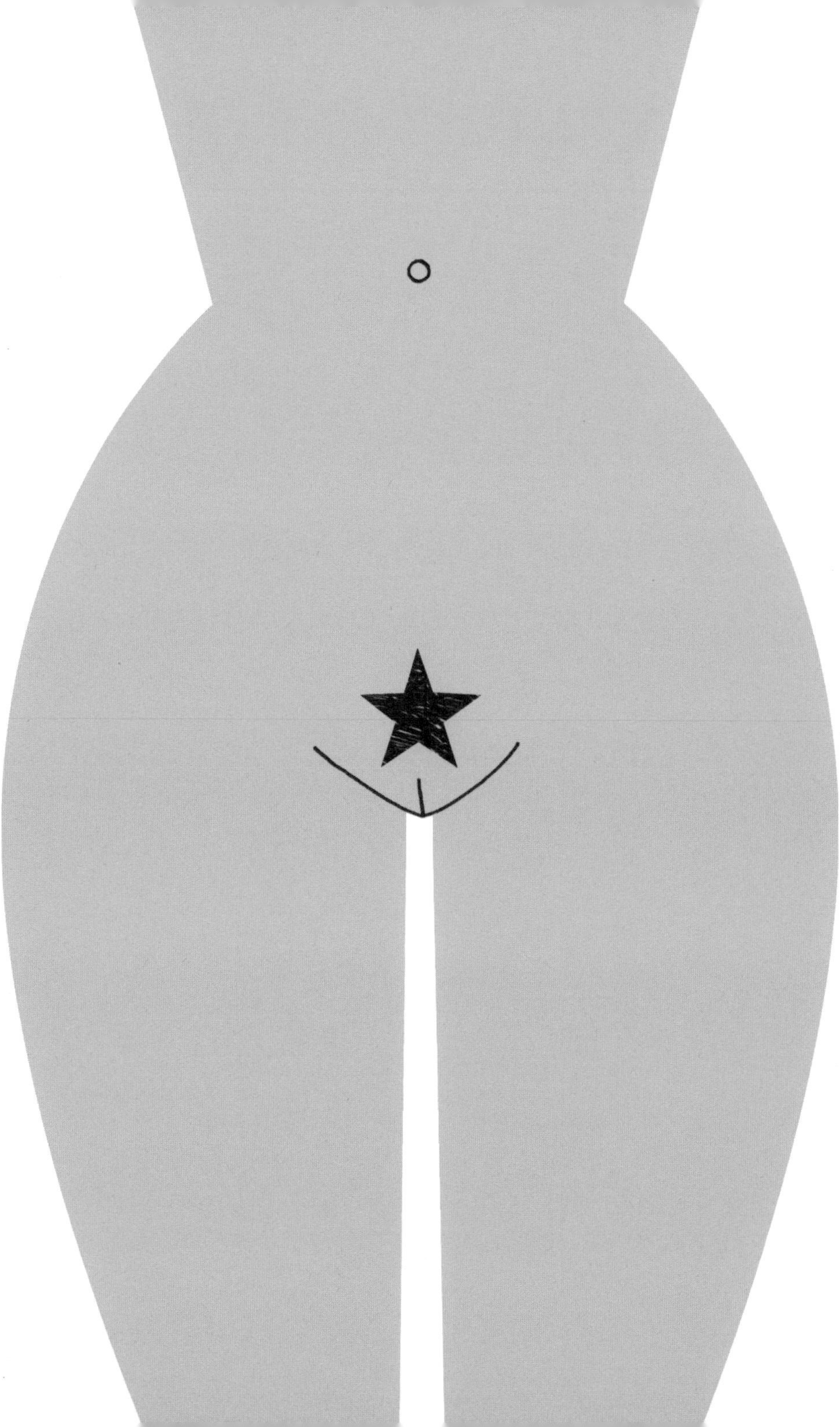

THE WINE GLASS

"We are all mortal until the first kiss and the second glass of wine."

                              Eduardo Galeano

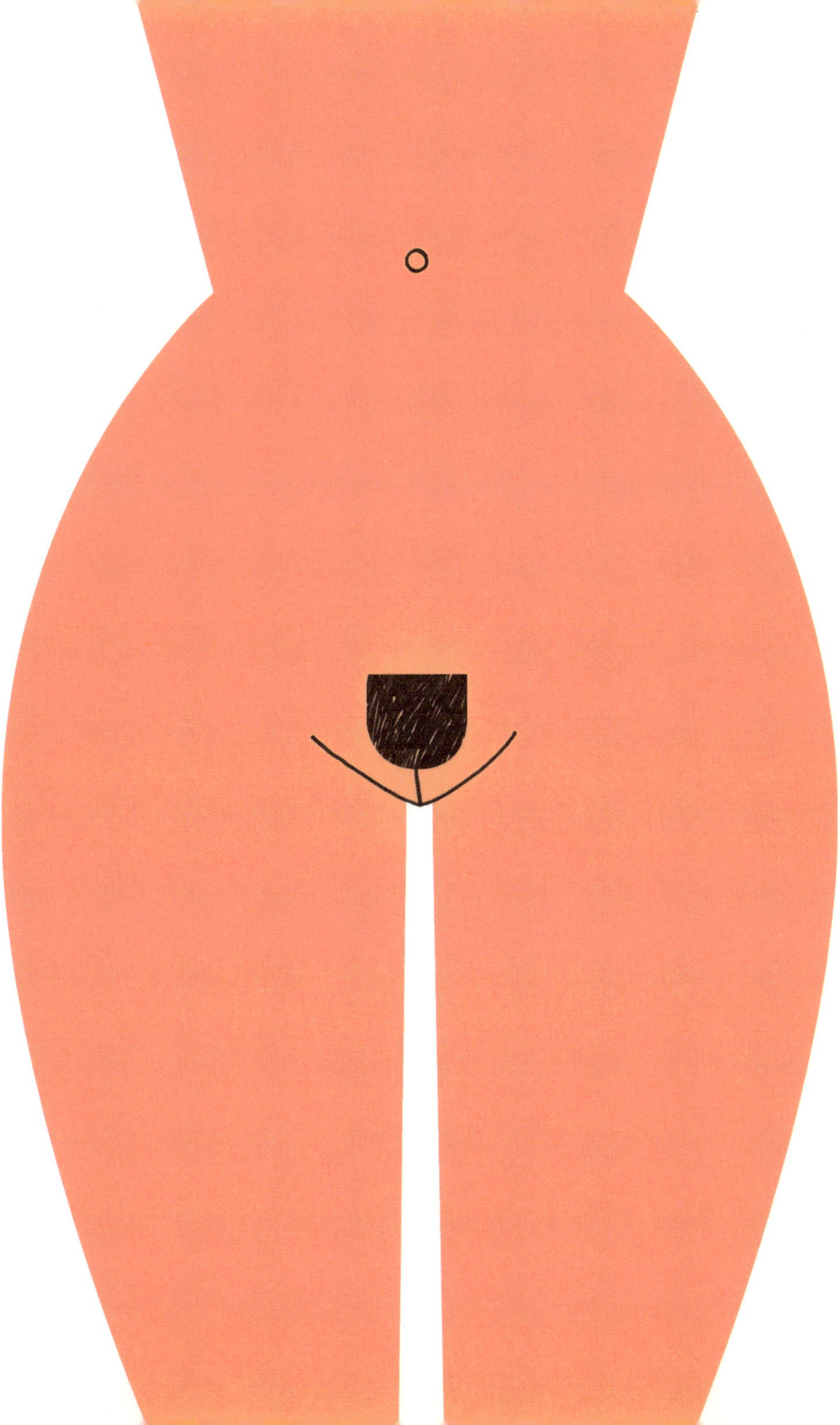

THE ZEUS

"Open your mouth and shut your eyes and see what Zeus will send you."

Aristophanes

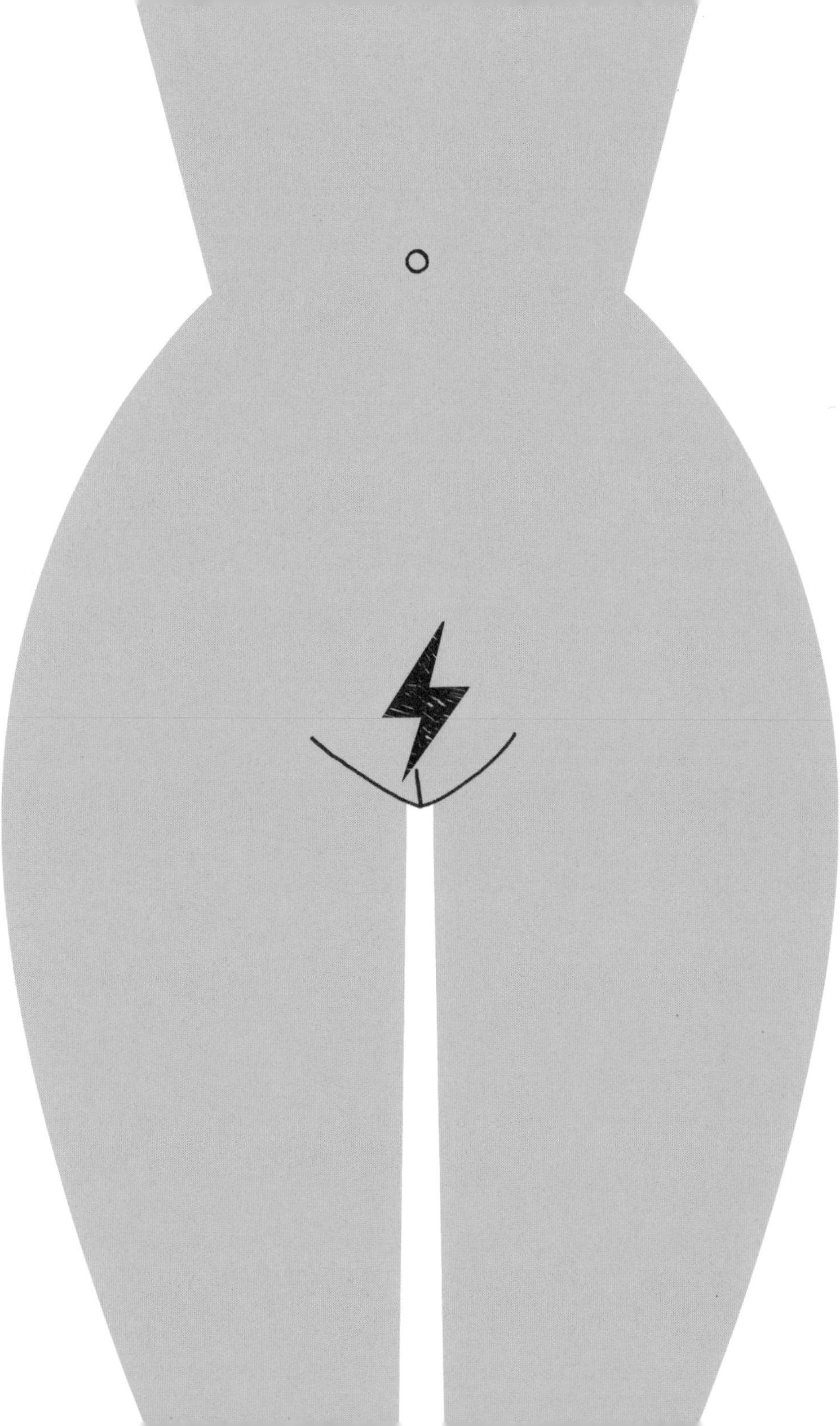

THIS WAY

"Some Cupid kills with arrows, some with traps."
                                            Shakespeare

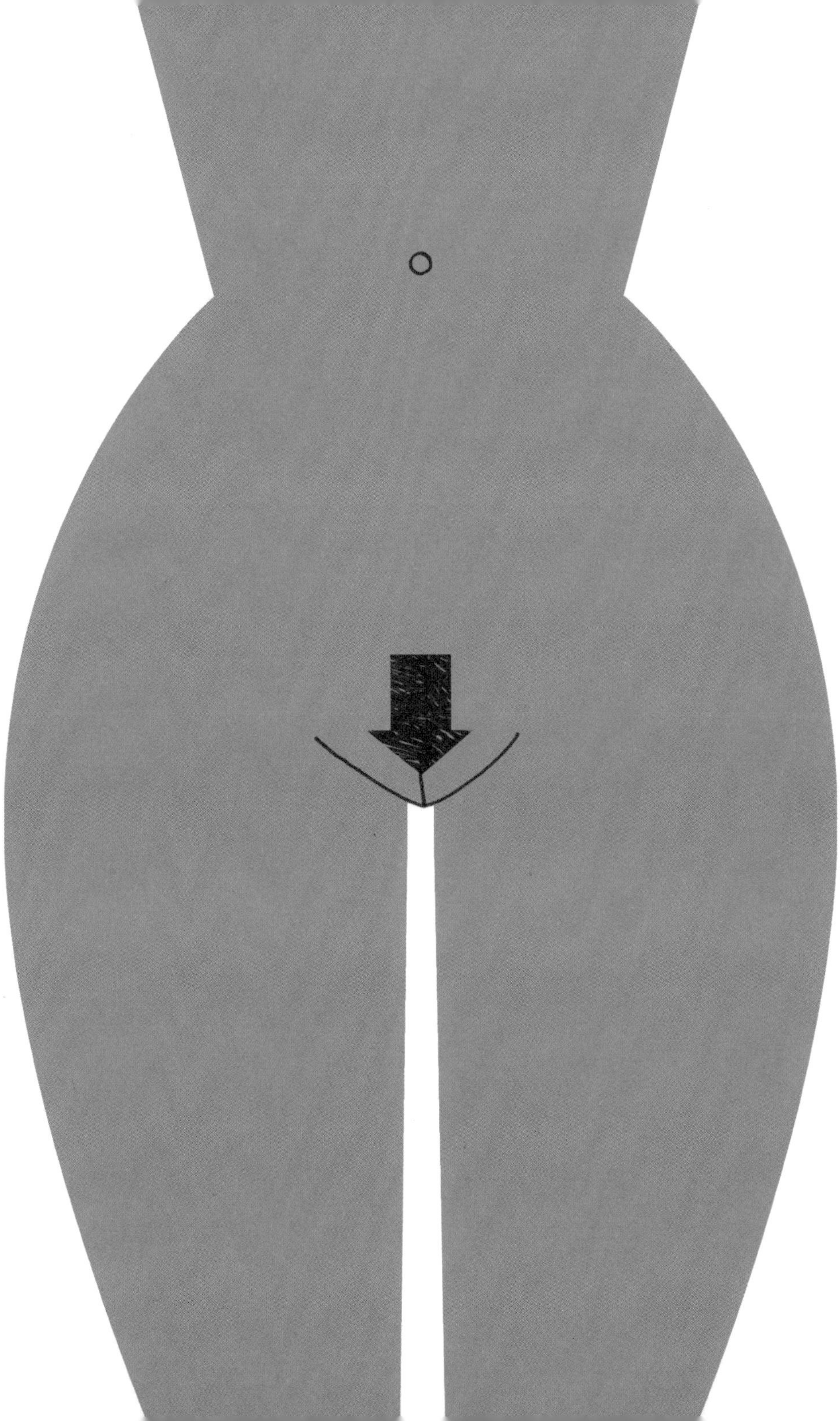

THE BUTTERFLY

"'i almost wish we were butterflies and liv'd but three summer days three such days with you i could fill with more delight than fifty common years could ever contain."

John Keats

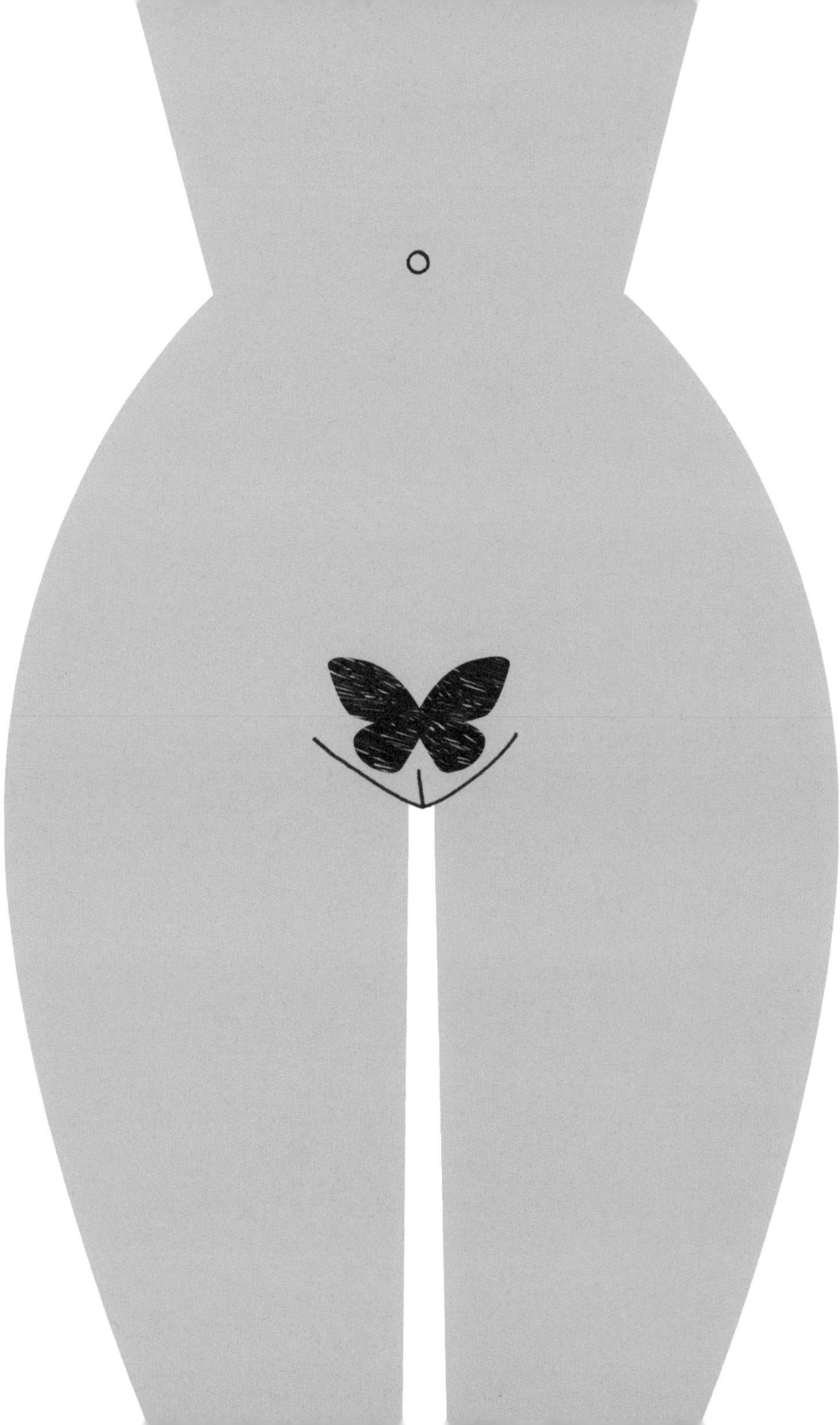

THE DIAMOND

"It's tacky to wear diamonds before you're forty..."
Truman Capote

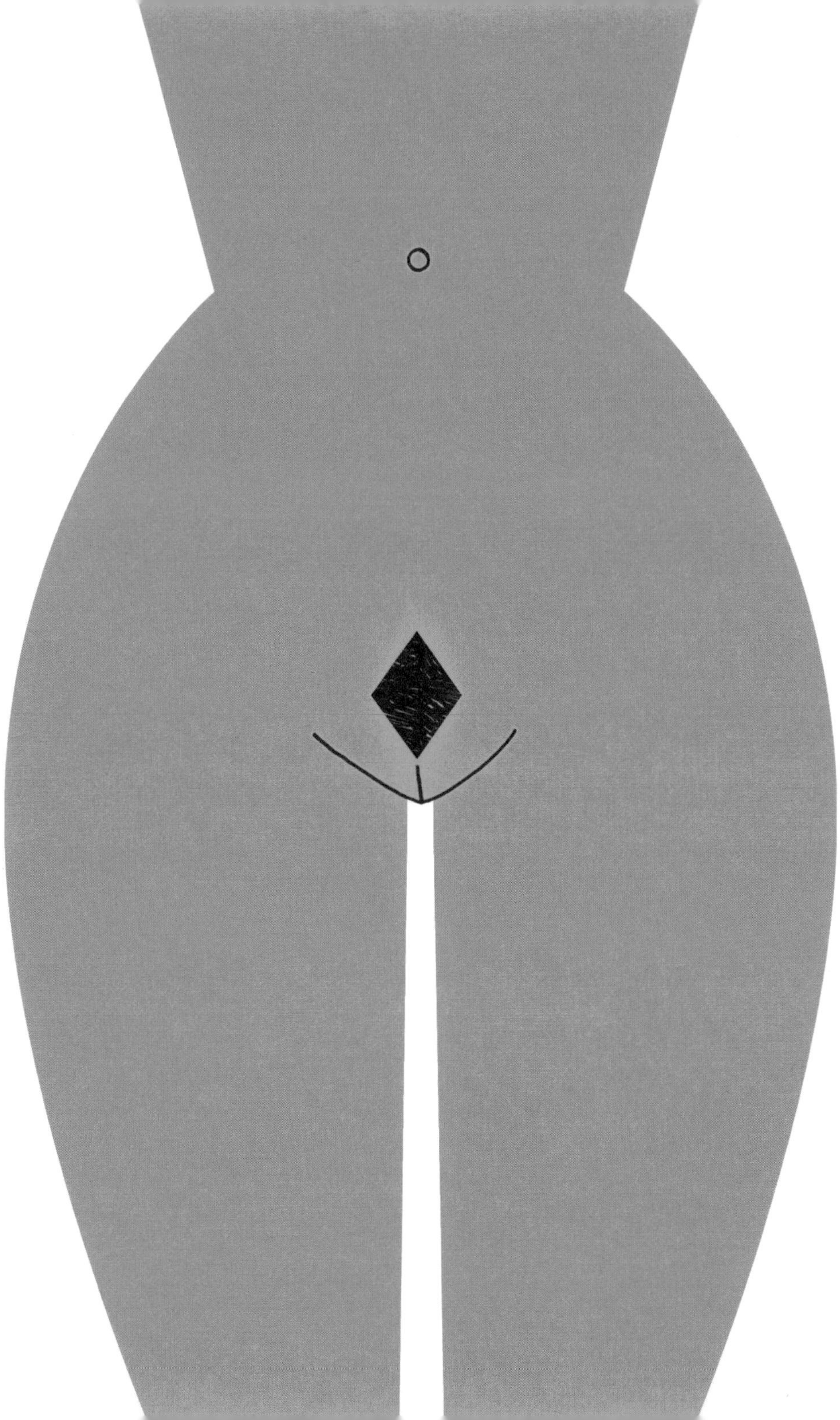

THE FiRST AiD

"i know a man who gave up smoking, drinking, sex, and rich food. He was healthy right up to the day he killed himself."

Johnny Carson

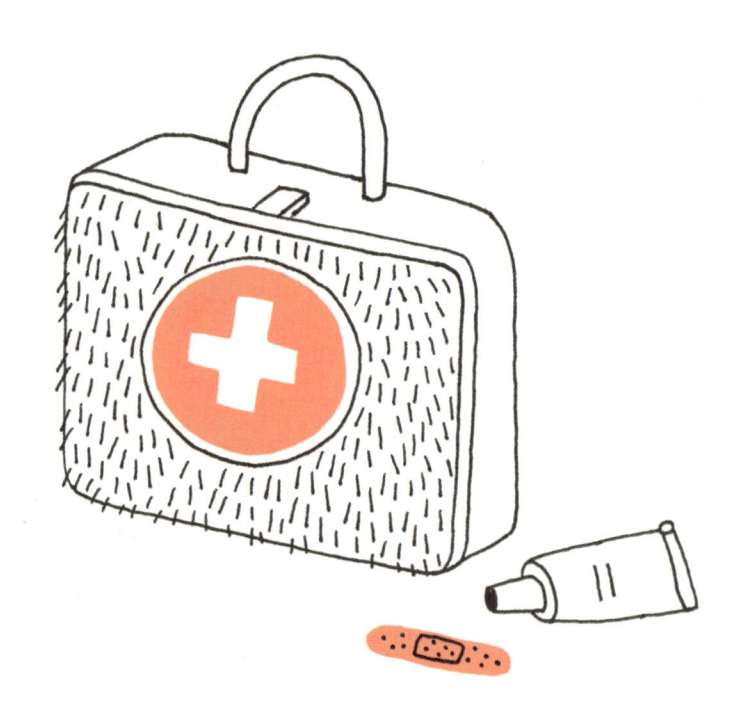

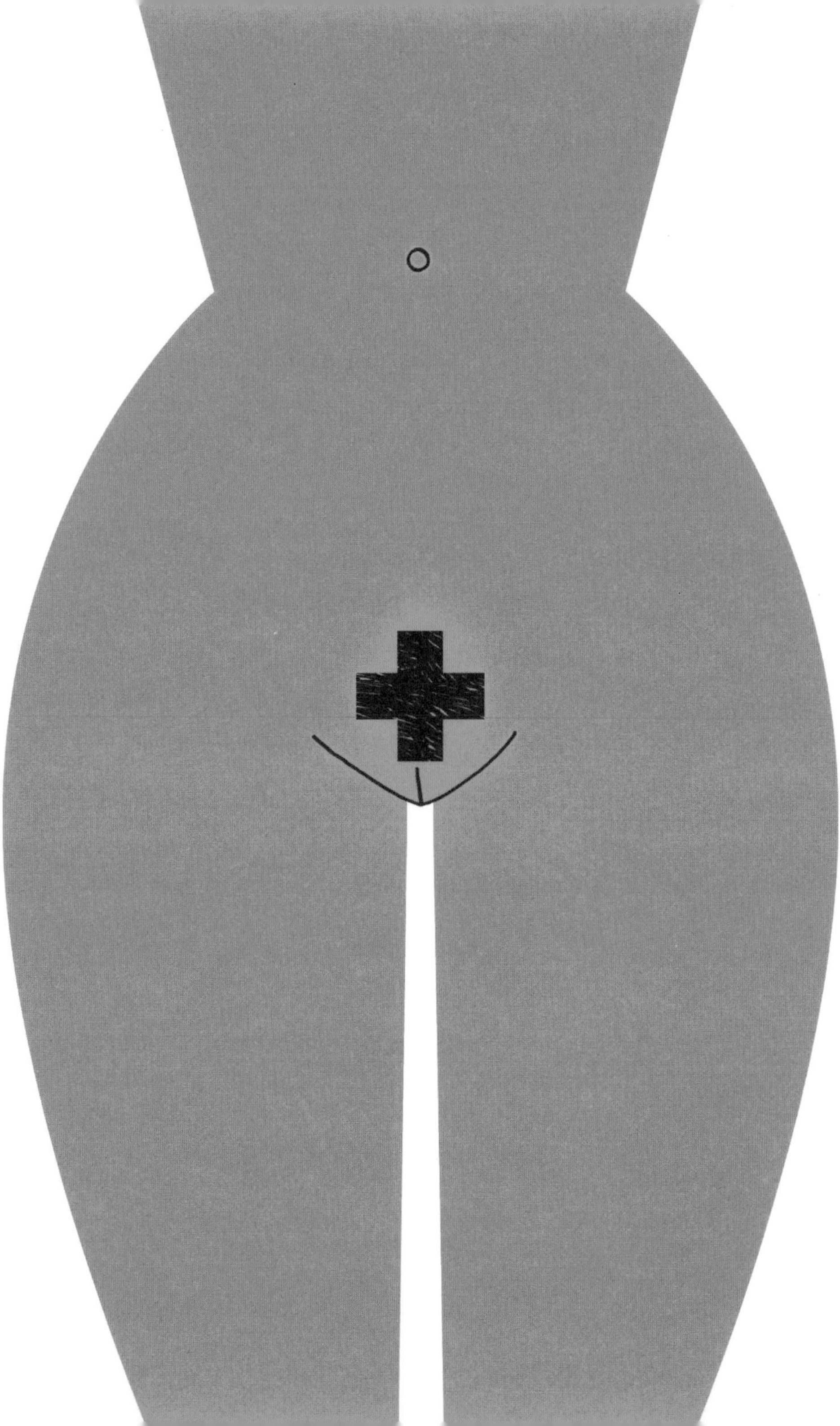

THE FLOWER

"The flower is the poetry of reproduction. it is an example of the eternal seductiveness of life."

                                    Jean Giraudoux

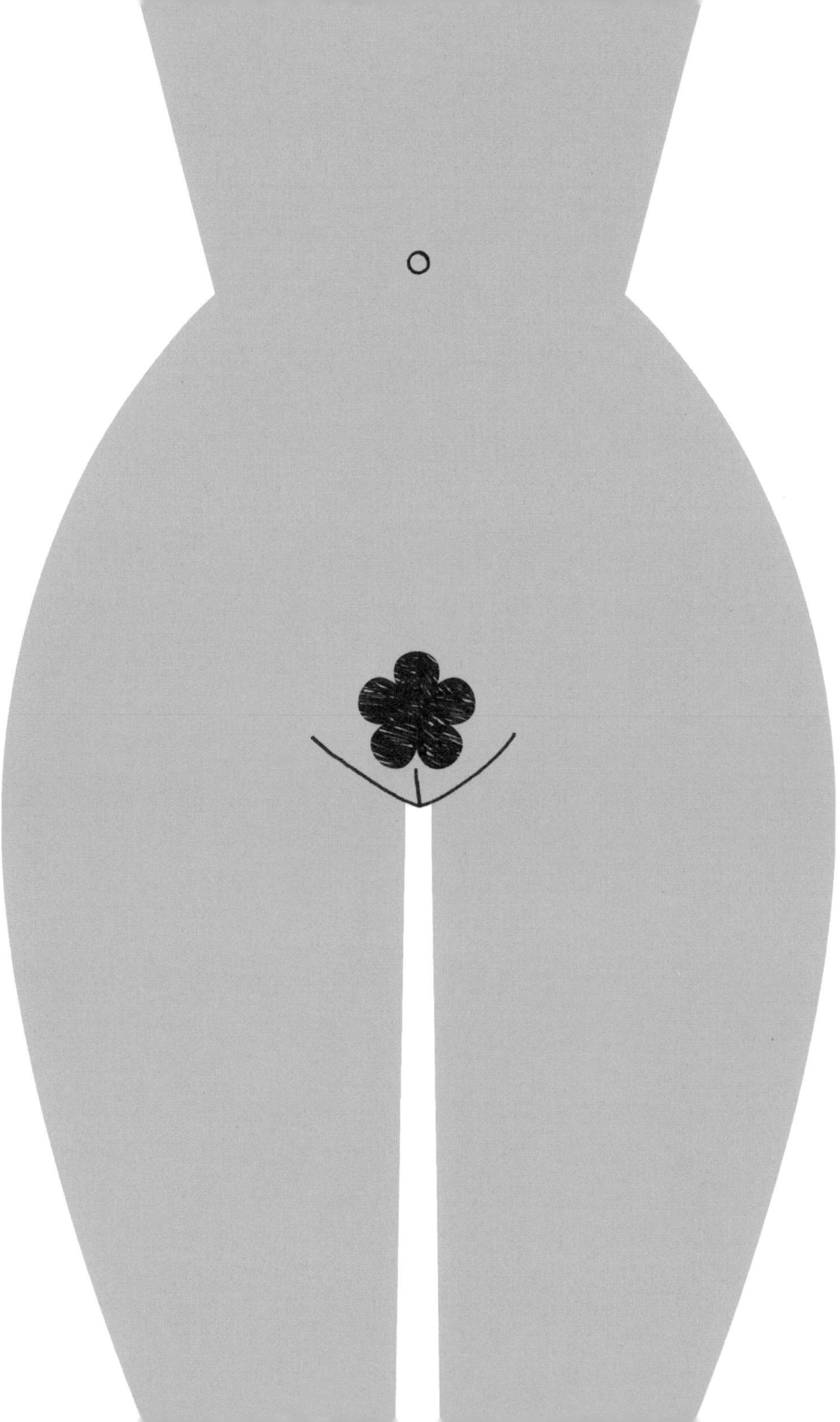

THE MOUSTACHE

"Kissing a man with a beard is a lot like going to a picnic. You don't mind going through a little bush to get there!"

                                            Minnie Pearl

THE PEACE & LOVE

"The more we sweat in peace the less we bleed in war."

      Vijaya Lakshmi Pandit

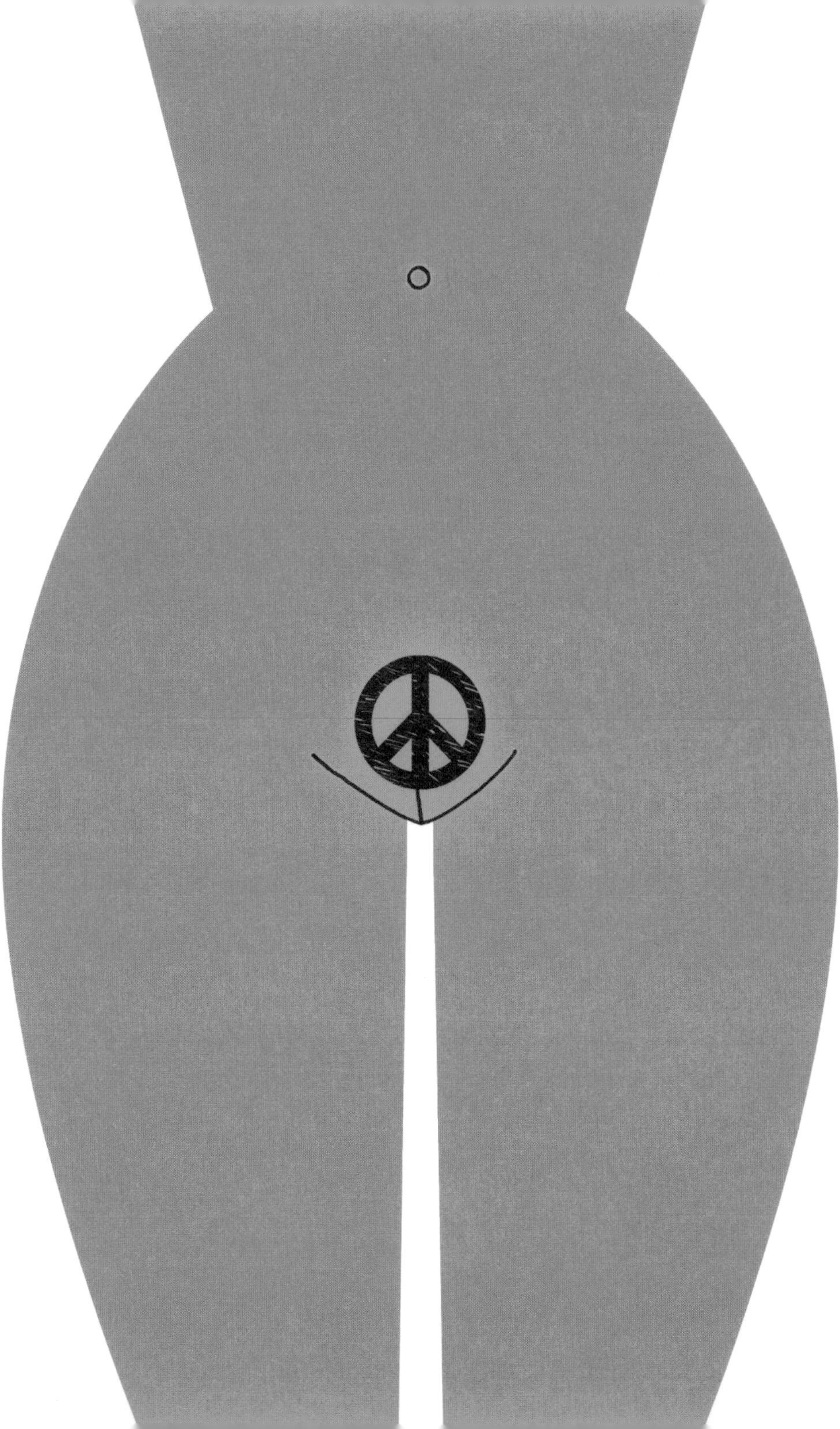

THE SPOOR

"The only thing of importance, when we depart, will be the traces of love we have left behind."

Albert Schweitzer

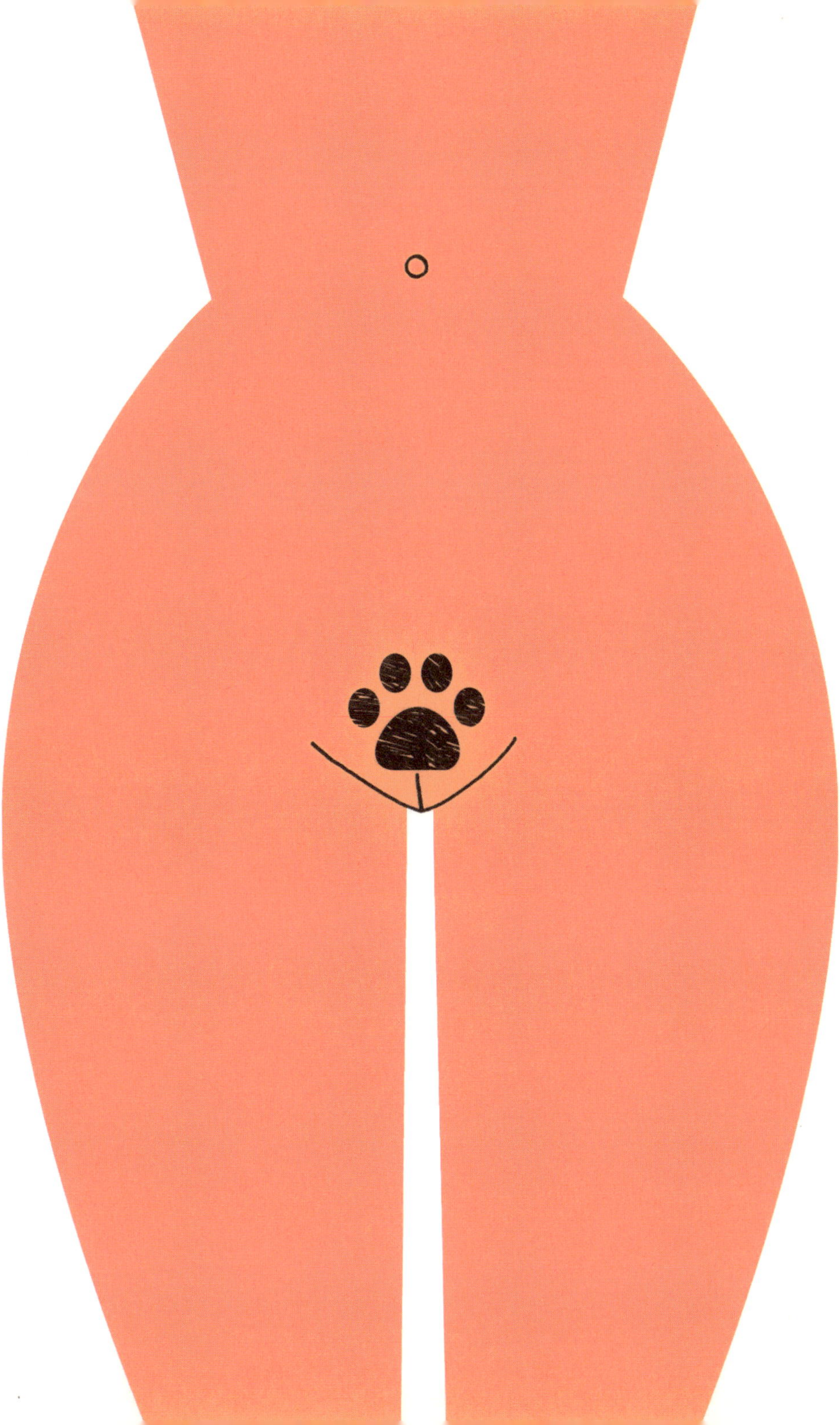

THE SUN

"The feathery curtains stretching o'er the sun's bright couch..."

        Percy Bysshe Shelley

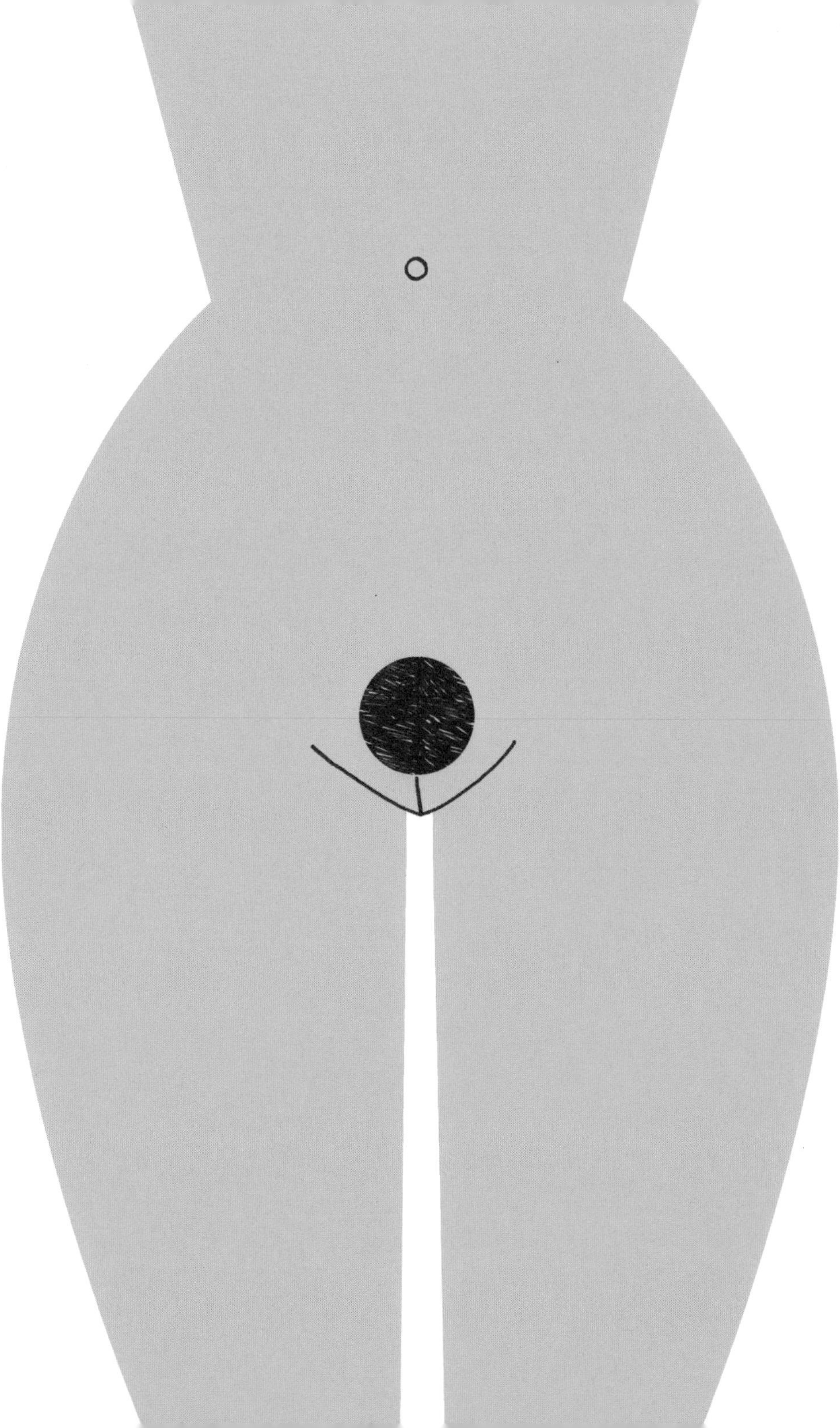

MY WAY

"And now, the end is here. And so i face the final curtain. My friend, i'll say it clear. i'll state my case, of which i'm certain. i've lived a life that's full. i traveled each and ev'ry highway. And more, much more than this, i did it my way."

Frank Sinatra

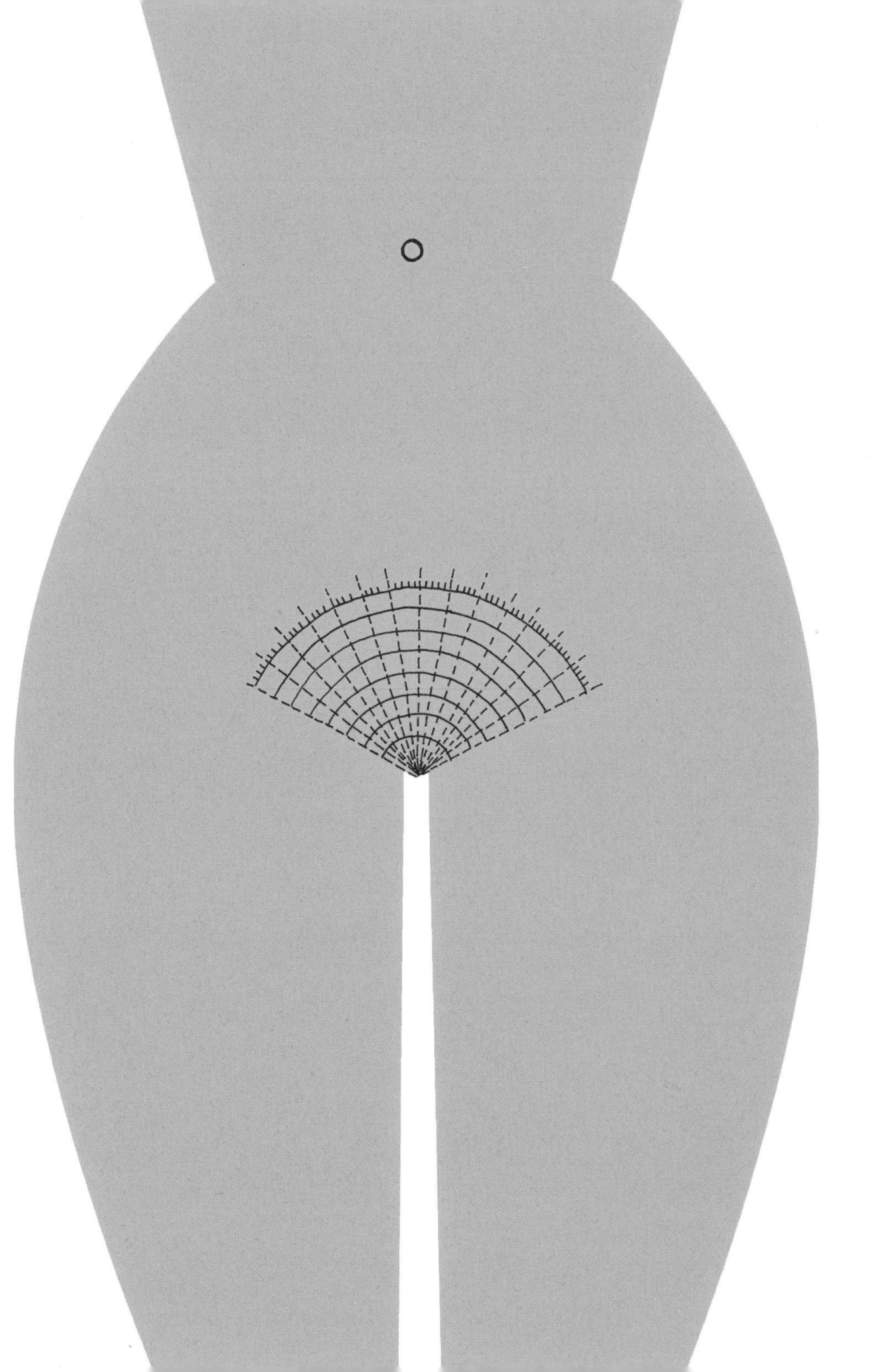

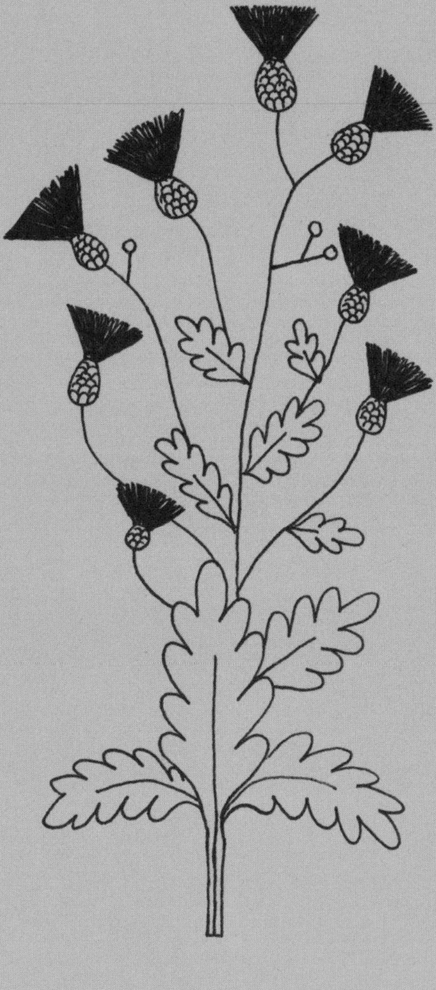

THE END

ABOUT THE AUTHOR
Caroline Selmes

French illustrator, former art director in advertising agencies. She worked in Paris, Barcelona, Madrid, and she is now living in London.
When she is not drawing, she is travelling the world, dancing salsa, scuba-diving, cooking vegetarian food, making ceramics, and drinking wine.
Caroline recently published for Lunwerg *Muerte a Los Hombre Malos*.

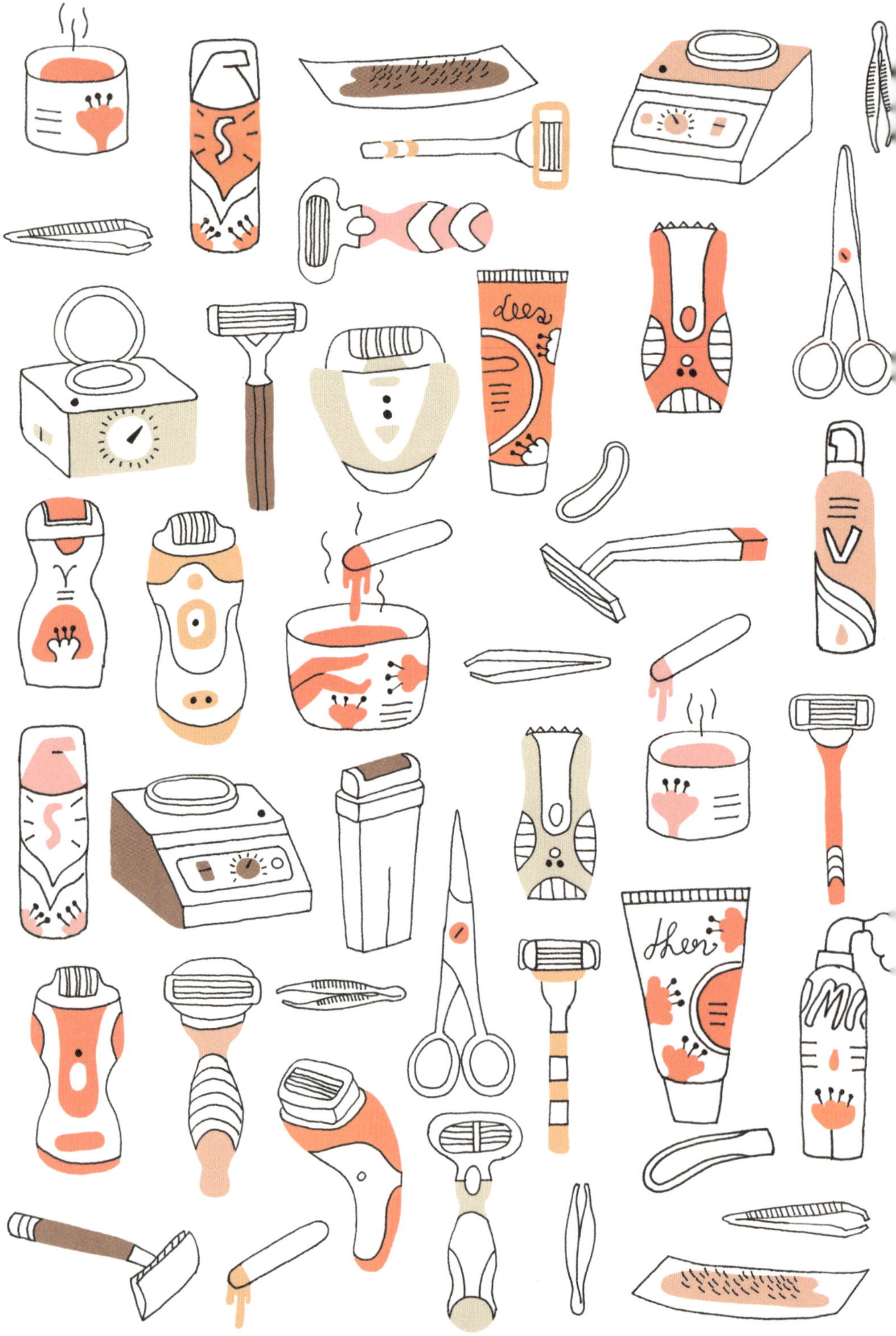
dees
Ther